Edward Jewitt Robinson

Reports of Brand's breech-loading military fire arm

Edward Jewitt Robinson

Reports of Brand's breech-loading military fire arm

ISBN/EAN: 9783337728397

Printed in Europe, USA, Canada, Australia, Japan

Cover: Foto ©ninafisch / pixelio.de

More available books at **www.hansebooks.com**

REPORTS OF
Brand's Breech-Loading
MILITARY
FIRE ARM,
MANUFACTURED BY E. ROBINSON,

Nos. 120, 122, 124 & 126 Wooster Street,

NEW YORK.

Who has the exclusive right to manufacture the Arm, both for Military
and Sporting purposes.

NEW YORK, MARCH 30th, 1863.

NEW YORK:
ISAAC J. OLIVER, STEAM BOOK AND JOB PRINTER,
32 Beekman Street.

1863.

PREFACE.

In presenting the following flattering opinions of my breech-loading fire arms to the public, I wish to acknowledge the kind consideration with which I have been universally received by the distinguished officers and gentlemen, whose attention has been freely given whenever asked; and the interest shown by the officers of army and navy departments in all improvements in fire arms, which tend to render our army and navy more efficient is sufficient proof that these gentlemen desire only the good of the country, and that they are only anxious that the best weapons should be adopted by the government.

In order that these arms may be understood by the readers of the following pages, it is necessary that I should give a general description of their construction and operation, as well as of the amunition used, which we will do as briefly as possible.

The arm is of the class called breech-loaders, and the amunition used is what is called fixed, (a copper case containing the powder, fulminate, and ball, water tight and safe from injury or accident.) The barrel of the rifle is of the same bore and length as the Springfield rifle musket, but the grooves of the rifling are of a peculiar shape and twist found only in guns made be me. To the barrel is attached what is called a receiver made of best wrought iron, containing a sliding breech in which is the lock and all its connections. This sliding breech is drawn back to insert the cartridge by a knuckle joint lever, which, when closed by the grasp of the hand is entirely encased in the receiver. The guard is similar to that of the Springfield musket, and there are no levers under the arm to catch the accoutrements of the soldier.

The barrel and receiver when connected and containing the lock and breech piece, make a complete arm without the wood of the stock, and can be fired in this state without difficulty, whereas, the Springfield musket depends entirely on the stock for support. The sliding breech with the lock can be removed by taking out one screw, and this could be done by the soldier on the field of battle, and replaced without trouble. A charge cannot be fired unless the breech is closed, and the breech cannot be closed unless all is right, and the whole operation is so simple that the most stupid cannot make a mistake.

The barrel is so constructed that the ball in passing through does not leave any lead in the rifle grooves, nor get sufficiently foul to injure the range, both of which causes operate in most arms to make poor shots.

The receiver is so arranged that either a rifle or smooth bore barrel can be put in at pleasure, and with the smooth bore we use our new metallic cartridge of the same size and character as the rifle cartridge, but containing buck shot, wad, and round ball. The ball being larger than the bore of the barrel prevents all windage, and gives great force and accuracy to this kind of amunition.

As the sliding breech is operated entirely from the top of the arm, and since there are no levers underneath to catch the equipments of the soldier, one of the most serious objections to breech-loading fire arms is obviated, and he is enabled to load in any position, and to go through the regular drill with ease and precision.

I think now that I have said enough to give a general idea of the improvements, and I feel satisfied that further inspection will prove that they possess great merit, and add the favorable opinions of all to the testimony of the distinguished generals who have given it so thorough and severe tests. With these remarks I leave the reader to peruse the following pages, and to form his own opinion.

EDWARD ROBINSON.

BOSTON, Nov. 10, 1862.

E. ROBINSON, ESQ.,
126 Wooster Street, New York.

DEAR SIR : I learn that you have large facilities for the manufacture of fire-arms. I have a breech-loading [fire-arm which I
consider the best at the present time in existence, which I should
like you to manufacture. I will give you the exclusive license if
we can agree upon terms.

Yonrs respectfully,

E. G. ALLEN.

---

126 WOOSTER STREET, N. Y.
Nov. 12, 1862.

COL. E. G. ALLEN.

DEAR SIR : Bring your gun. If it is what you claim for it, I will
make arrangements with you for the exclusive right to manufacture the arm under the patent. The country should not be one day
without it, if it is superior to those now in use.

Yours respectfully,

E. ROBINSON.

BOSTON, March 26, 1863.

EDWARD ROBINSON,
Armory, No. 120 to 126 Wooster Street, New York.

DEAR SIR : In answer to your inquiries in regard to your rights,
titles and interests to manufacture and sell, the several and all
improvements and inventions in Breech-Loading Fire Arms, mode
of rifling guns and improvements for Cartridges for the same invented and patented, or being patented by E. G. Allen, and C. C.
Brand, your exclusive license, dated December 8, 1862, from E.
G. Allen and A. N. Clark, gives you full power to manufacture, or
cause to be manufactured, all Fire Arms, (excepting those known
as Pistols,) under any or all patents and improvements made by C.
C. Brand. Said Brand having conveyed to the undersigned on Sep-

tember 13, 1862, the full and exclusive right as above. and I, E. G. Allen, having conveyed to you on the 8, day of December, 1862, all of my said improvements and inventions by a license, the full and exclusive right to manufacture and sell within the limits of the United States. ₍Trusting that the above will be perfectly satisfactory to your inquiries, both to yourself and to the, public,

Respectfully, your obedient servants,

E. G. ALLEN,
A. N. CLARK.

———

HEADQUARTERS, NEAR WASHINGTON, D. C.,
October 22d, 1862.

COL. E. G. ALLEN, Washington, D. C.

DEAR SIR : The breech-loading rifle musket, known as Allen & Brand patent, has been placed in my hands for examination and experiment, and from the former, I feel no hesitation in pronouncing it to be the best breech-loading weapon I have seen. I have had no opportunity to try it, but from the well known character of those who have reported the results, I am almost as well satisfied as though the experiments had been made by myself. Breech loading weapons are an improvement on the old style of arms, as they afford greater facility in loading and greater rapidity of fire, and when these advantages are attained, at no sacrifice in accuracy, or less complication in the construction in the arms, it appears to me to be expedient to adopt them. Again I say it is the best arm of the character I have seen, and a greater improvement on the arms in use—I mean the Springfield musket.

Yours truly,   JOSEPH HOOKER.
Major General.

———

U. S. NAVY YARD,
Washington, July 1, 1862.

CAPT. A. A. HARWOOD,
Chief of Bureau of Ordnance and Hydro.

SIR : As directed, an examination has been made of a breech-loading musket, invented by Mr. Brand and presented by Colonel Allen. The report of trial is enclosed herewith.

The arm is remarkably compact and solid in the breech-loading apparatus. The plug which closes the breech, contains the lock, so that there is no external projection, as usual at that part.

The apparatus works rearward of the barrel in the neck of the stock, and unless the lever is down and closes the barrel perfectly, the lock *will not act*, and there is also the advantage that the grip of the hand naturally shuts the lever close down, if not so already. The piece was fired one hundred and eighty-five times, and looks capable of *any endurance.*

The low comparative charge and recoil, gives the piece remarkable steadiness in aim.'

I have the honor to be

Very respectfully, your obedient servant,

[Signed]   JOHN A. DAHLGREN.

Commandant.

———

ORDINANCE OFFICE, June 30, 1862.

CAPTAIN J. A. DAHLGREN, Commandant.

SIR : In obedience to your orders I have examined and tested the Brands Patent Breech-loading Rifle musket, presented by Col. E. G. Allen, of Boston, and have to submit the following report. The weight and measurement were found to be as follows :

Weight of gun complete (with ramrod)............13.30 lbs*

Weight of barrel,................................5.72 lbs.

Weight of stock,.................................6.84 lbs,

Length of barrel,................................37 in.

Diameter of bore,.............................37.17 "

Number of grooves,............................... .5

Width,   "   .... .15 inch

Depth,   "   .... .15 "

Number of lands,............................... 5

Twist—the first ten inches regular at one turn in......52½ in.

It then increases to the muzzle, to one turn in..........32 in.

A solid breech plate encloses the end of the barrel, breech-plate connecting link and lever. The breech piece encloses the lock ; a guide pin projects from its forward face and enters the breech-

* Error 12.56 lbs. Weight only 9.46 lbs. · [See Second Report, page 26.]

plate, and a clutch on each side of forward face receives the copper cylinder, and holds it securely by the rim. The point of the hammer plays through a slot in the upper edge of breech-piece as in Colt's rifle. The lever works on top, the lifting end coming just abaft the hammer, with a catch-spring on the end, worked by the thumb. The recoil is transmitted through the joints to the large screw on after end of lever, the upward strain checked by the guide-pin and clutches mentioned above.

The trial commenced on the 28th inst., first for penetration. Ten rounds were fired at a target two feet square, made of pine boards, about $1\frac{1}{8}$ inches thick, and $1\frac{1}{8}$ inches apart, 116 yards distant, resulting as follows :

4 passed through 1st board.

2	"	"	2d	Clear of cross pieces, 2 in wake of them	
2	"	"	3d	" " 2 " "	
2	"	"	4th	" " 2 " "	
3	"	"	5th	(One of above coming clear.)	
3	"	"	6th		
2	"	"	7th	1 Lodging.	
2	"	"	8th		
1	"	"	9th		
1	"	"	10th		
1	"	"	11th		

Total thickness, 11 13-16 inches solid, through boards and cross pieces—8 11-16 inches.

Average weight of three cartridges : charge, 38 gns.; balls, 497 gns.; metallic case, 37 gns. Total—572 gns.

For comparison ten rounds were fired with a Springfield musket of 58, at a similar target, with results as follows :

6 passed through 1st board, clear of cross pieces, 2 in their wake.
6 passed through 2d board, clear of cross pieces, 2 in wake of them.

6	"	"	3d	"	"	
6	"	"	4th	"	"	
6	"	"	5th	"	"	
5	"	"	6th	"	"	
5	"	"	7th	"	"	
4	"	"	8th	"	" 1 Lodging.	
4	"	"	9th	"	"	
4	"	"	10th	"	"	
1	"	"	11th	"	" 1 Lodging.	
1	Indenture in	12th	"	"		

Total thickness—11 12-16 inch through solid; 9, thickness 9 10-16 inch. Average weight of cartridge—charge, 60 gns.; ball, 530 gns. Total—590 gns.

June 20th, P. M., 50 rounds were fired on time by Mr. Allen, who is familiar with the arm, sitting at rest and aiming, making very good shots.

Time, 9· 18·· temperature before firing ; air 83½°, Gun, 82½· After firing, air 83½°, gun 124°.

Fifty rounds were then fired by Mr. Buttingham, (unused to the piece), in same manner, making very good shots.

Time, 10· 10·· temperature before firing, air 83½· Gun, 103½ after firing, air 83½° Gun 136°.

Twenty-five rounds were then fired by Mr. Allen, standing and aiming off-hand at line of piles. Time, 4· 35·· temperature before firing : air, 84°, gun 99°; after firing, air 81°, gun 119°.

Twenty-five rounds were then fired by Mr. Buttingham in same way. Time, 4· 20·· temperature before firing. Air 86°, gun 108°. After firing, air 87°, gun 130°.

At this time (160 rounds) the gun was washed out, it was found to be very dirty, but not leaded, which is owing (Mr. Allen says)to the edges of the grooves being curved.

June 30th, 5 rounds for escape of gas, slight traces on two papers and evidence of some escape outside of three cylinders.

Twenty rounds were then fired for accuracy at a target 2 feet square, 116 yards distant, ten by Mr. Allen and ten by Mr. Buttingham. Wind moderate, quartering, 18 shots struck the target ; mean distance from center of bull's eye 5.3 in ; 3 shots struck the bull's eye 5 inches in diameter.

For comparison, 20 rounds were fired by Mr. Buttingham with pringfield musket 1858, under same conditions, 20 shot struck the target, mean distance from bull's eye, 6. 3 in. No shot struck the bull's eye.

The number of cartridges presented being limited, only 185 rounds were fired, so there was not a fair test for endurance.

From the above tests it appears that for *penetration, certainty of firing, and for accuracy, this is very superior musket.*

Though the balls take the grooves at once there is but little escape of gas. The works resist the recoil very well. The cylinder shell has to be removed by the finger.

The works moved stifly during the whole trial, binding on the sides, and on the two guide screws, though the latter were eased twice. This binding could of course be avoided in other pieces made hereafter.

The piece must be half cocked before inserting a cartridge, and half cocked also before removing the cylinder shell after firing, both of which Mr. Allen claims to be advantageous.

The head of the lever is inconvenient for grasping with a greasy thumb and finger, but a better form could be readily adopted. After firing the above 185 times, the strap or lever part of the breech piece was found to be broken on both sides of the trigger in wake of trigger pin. The strap can of course be made strong enough in other pieces to resist all strain upon it.

The balls were conical as usual. The cylinders inclosing the fulminate in the arm were made by machinery, and very rarely failed.   Respectfully submitted,

(Signed,)   ROBERT L. MAY,
Lieut. U. S. N.

WASHINGTON, D. C., Oct. 24, 1862.
BRG. GEN. RIPLEY,
       Chief of Ordnance.

DEAR SIR: I have carefully examined Allen's breech loading rifle, a new patented arm, and though I have not seen it tried, I am satisfied from its construction, and the certificates of officers who have tried it, that it must be a valuable weapon.

The rifle, the bayonet, and the cartridge, all strike me as the best of their kind that I have seen, and should they stand the test required by Government, I cannot but think that the introduction of this new arm into our service would be a great desideratum.   Very respectfully,

RUFUS KING,
Brig. Gen. Volunteers.

BOSTON, Sept. 15, 1862.
COL. E. G. ALLEN.

DEAR SIR: You know I have always detested breach-loading rifles. I have tried a great many, which confirmed my belief. I have tried yours. I have tried it over 100 times. I have examined it as carefully as I am able, and I say now I think well of your gun.

I think for *simplicity, certainty,* and wear, it is incomparably the best and only decent breech-loader I have ever seen.

If the Government will examine and test your gun fully, they will take it in preference to any gun they have ever used.

I know this, and I congratulate you as being influential in getting up a gun which is to be *the* gun for the future.

Keep this and tell me two years from now whether I am right.

Yours truly,

W. D. NORTHERD.

———

HEADQUARTERS 3D BRIGADE, 1ST DIVISION, 3D CORPS,
Oct. 19th, 1862.

SIR : I deem it my duty to signify to you my approbation of your truly valuable breech-loading rifle. I have examined many breech-loaders, but have never seen one that I regard so simple in construction, so easily comprehended, and so little liable to get out of order in the hands of inexperienced men as this gun of yours. The great rapidity with which it can be fired, the absence of heat at the chamber, the protection of the main parts from the effects of the weather, have all my admiration. I regard it as the best weapon of the kind I have ever seen.

I would add further, that I see no reason why the rawest recruit may not be learned to fully understand this arm and the use of it with as great rapidity, and in as short a space of time, as would be necessary to teach him to use any one of the weapons now in use in the army.

I am, sir, respectfully yours,

H. G. BARRY,

COL. E. G. ALLEN,   Brig. Gen. Volunteers.
WASHINGTON, D. C.,

———

WASHINGTON, D. C., Oct. 20, 1862.

COL. E. G. ALLEN.

SIR : Having been present this afternoon at the experimental firing of your breech-loading rifle, I have no hesitation in saying that, in my judgment, the arm is superior for some purposes in the field to that of any other breech-loading fire-arm that I have ever seen.

The novel construction of the breech—simplicity, strength, and apparent durability—would seem to contain all the requisites that may be required for small arms for field service, with a charge of only 38 grains of powder. At an elevation of only 2½ degrees, the balls of 572 grains were repeatedly thrown a distance of 1,200 yards.

Hoping that Government will encourage merit, I hope that you will receive an order to furnish some on their account.

Very truly yours,
GEN. EBENEZER H. STONE.

BOSTON, Sept. 24, 1862.

HON. P. H. WATSON.

DEAR SIR : Col. E. G. Allen, who, I think you know, has a breech-loading musket which I think has great merit, and deserves the attention of the officers of the Government.

If possible for you to do so, I hope you will examine it personally and aid him to bring it to the attention of the proper office.

Yours truly,
D. W. GOOCH, M. C.

NEW YORK, Oct. 2, 1862.

COL. E. G. ALLEN.

DEAR SIR : We take great pleasure in informing you that we have examined and tested your new arm, and in stating that, in our judgment, it is superior to any rifle we have ever tested.

We are particularly struck with the simplicity of construction, accuracy of aim, and absence of recoil in discharge ; and, indeed, in all its details, challenges our admiration.

Very truly yours,
TIFFANY & CO.

15

Boston, Sept. 22, 1862.

Col. E. G. Allen.

Dear Sir : I will now state, in writing, in accordance with your request, the impressions I entertain of the new breech-loading rifle, placed by you in my hands for examination and use. I have fired and seen it fired about one hundred times, most of the shots being for target practice, a few of them being made to enable me to observe the range of the balls and the effects of firing over the water in " ricochet."

I think your rifle has substantial merit in the following, among other, particulars :

1st. It has the inestimable advantage of being a breech-loader, while it seems to me to avoid most, if not all, the dangers and inconveniences of that kind of weapon.

It also uses the metallic cartridge, with percussion powder. In the *rim* which projects from the rear end the powder is enclosed and hermetically sealed, and the ball itself forming the front end of the cartridge ! There can be no mistake in the use of it ; it cannot go in wrong end foremost ; there is no biting off one end of it required ; there is no chance of forgetting powder, or ball, or cap ; they go altogether right end foremost, and there can be nothing left in the barrel after firing that can set fire to the succeeding charge. The amunition is in the best form for safety, certainty, convenience, and rapid use. It is least liable to accidental wet, heat, or combustion ; and the annealed copper of which the case is made avoids the most dangerous and destructive characteristic of ordinary breech-loaders, viz.: that of leaking gas at the breech soon after they are put in use.

2d. After the first charge has been fired the copper case cannot be easily removed without half-cocking the lock, and this peculiarity is important to prevent mistakes. How much soever the marksman may be excited in action, before he can get rid of the copper case which held the charge he has already fired off, he must half-cock his lock, and by doing that he necessarily *secures himself* from any *accidental explosion* of the *succeeding charge*. The proper succession of movements by the soldier does not depend on his presence of mind, but is made necessary by the operation of the mechanism itself.

3d. The resistance to the recoil of the charge is transmitted through the breech to the body of the gun in a peculiar way ;

and this breech, though moveable forward and back, is, when in place, about as firm as though it were cast solid upon the barrel. This is owing to the way in which the levers are so connected by joints that their resistance to the recoil is transmitted in a line passing through the centre of the joints and centre of the levers to the stock itself.

4th. That part of the stock bearing the breech, lock, &c., is entirely of metal, and very compact. The lock is inside and out of sight ; the hammer central, and not on one side of the barrel ; and the entire mass of metal is in and around the breech of the gun, where it is best placed to resist the recoil by its "*vis inertiæ*," to balance the piece in the hand, to secure the most delicate parts from injury in service, and to preserve a clear space for the sights.

5th. Your rifle is so constructed that it can be rapidly loaded and discharged while the marksman is standing or laying in any position desirable, and with the least possible exposure of person, being in that respect superior—I think *superior* to several breech-loading carbines and rifles which have the breech and barrel hinged together.

6th. The parts seem solid and substantial, and easily separated, not fragile and delicate, as are some European breech-loaders.

7th. The recoil of your rifle seems to me less than others carrying the same weight of ball the same distance.

How much of this is owing to the smaller charge which is required, (as shown by the experiments made by the Ordnance Department,) and how much to the acceleration of the twist, or to other circumstances, I have now no means of determining.

8th. I am told that your rifle can be manufactured, using steel for barrels, and the best of stock and workmanship for all parts, several dollars cheaper than Sharp's and other standard rifles of this class.

With these advantages, together with those shown in the report of Ordnance Department, I should think that the Government would earnestly desire to have your rifle introduced into the service, as I am confident they are ready ever to appreciate whatever seems to them to be meritorious.

Respectfully yours,
(Signed)   WILLIAM WHITING,
Now Solicitor to the War Department.

WEST POINT, July 22, 1862.

BRIG. GEN. J. W. RIPLEY, Chief of Ordnance,

Washington, D. C.

SIR : I have the honor to report the results of a trial made yes-terday with *Allen's breech-loading rifle.*

The arm presented was nearly of the length of an ordinary rifle-musket. Its calibre was 54–100 inches, but the thickness of the barrel increased the weight of the arm to 1¾ lbs. more than that of the Springfield rifle-musket.

The barrel is joined to the stock by two strong checks of mal-leable iron, and between the checks the bolt closing the breach is worked by a double lever or toggle-joint. The end of the bolt is provided with a clutch to hold the end or rim of the metallic car-tridge, so that in loading the cartridge is inserted in the clutch, then moved forward into the bore by the lever. The gun being fixed, the cartridge still held in the clutch is withdrawn by the act of opening the breech.

One hundred and sixty-eight rounds were fired in rapid succession without the slightest difficulty. The breech arrangements worked easily and safely, without clogging, throughout the firing. Not the least foulness was detected.

For *rapidity, the gun was fired ten rounds in forty-two seconds.* No target practice was attempted, *but the general accuracy of the firing was excellent.* The *metallic* cartridge used carried the percussion powder in the rim, thus dispensing with the percussion cap.

The powder in one of the cartridges used weighed 38 grains, and the bullet, when carefully weighed, 459 grains.

At proper elevation the bullet was thrown to the distance of a mile with this small charge of powder.

In my opinion the invention possesses much merit.

    (Signed)   T. V. BENET,

                       Captain of Ordnance.

Copy furnished COL. E. G. ALLEN,

         31 Devonshire street, Boston, Mass.

Boston, Sept. 30, 1862.

Col. E. G. Allen, Sir:—

I, William G. Langdon, of Boston, do hereby certify that I am by trade a Gunsmith, and that I have had much experience and practice in the manufactory, testing, and shooting of rifles and fire arms of all descriptions, and that I have been employed by the Governor and Council of Massachusetts to furnish rifles for volunteer companies, that I have examined and very thoroughly tested the new rifle invented by C. C. Brand, and have found by numerous trials of it, and do not hesitate to say that for simplicity, strength, and durability, it far surpasses any similar fire arm ever before examined or seen by me ; and the closing of its breech is so secured as to wholly prevent the escape of gas through the same. While the simplicity of its construction and operation renders it less liable to get out of order than other fire arms, and for military purposes, generally, I regard it as far superior to any other fire arm ever before invented or patented.

Respectfully yours,

WILLIAM G. LANGDON.

Headquarters, Army of the Potomac,
March 15th, 1863.

The undersigned, having examined partially the breech-loading arm and metallic cartridge of Mr. Allen, are of the opinion that his system of breech-loading is simple and efficacious, and eminently adapted for the use of light troops.

From the tests applied to the metallic cartridge, it is evident that for safety of transportation and facility of loading, it commends itself to the consideration of the authorities.

E. R. PRATT,
Lieut. Col. and Judge Advocate.

J. HALY CLUER,
Major 10th Infantry, U. S. A.

Washington, D. C., March, 1863.

Col. E. G. Allen,

Dear Sir: In compliance with your request I have witnessed and tested to-day, the firing of your breech-loading fire arms, (Allen & Brand's patent rifled musket, carbine, and smooth bore), with your cartridges for the same.

Three hundred rounds were fired in one hour in the different arms, and on examination of the several barrels they were found to be in a *perfect condition*, it seemed to me, to continue the firing for *any length of time*, there being no *leading* or *fouling* of the barrels, or *nealing* of *the lock parts* of the arms. The entire absence of any leading or fouling is owing to the peculiar rifling of the barrels, and the construction of the cartridges, which are inventions of great value.

The amount of powder in your cartridges being less than 44 grains or a little more than *one half the* amount used in the Springfield regulation musket, and carrying the ordinary weight of ball used in that arm.

With this small comparative amount of powder the range attained was from 300 yards to one mile distant, at a low elevation. The *range* and *accuracy both were perfect*, and almost *invaribly striking the object aimed at*, in every instance of the firing of the 300 rounds.

Your arm possesses the great advantage I see in no other arm in use, viz: It can be loaded at present arms by three motions without endangering the soldier, or it can with same saving of exposure, be loaded while laying flat on the ground. I consider these advantages of great importance, for it is a well known fact that a large per cent. of wounds received in battle are in the arms and hands while in the act of loading the arm known as the Springfield regulation musket, now in use, and other muzzel loading arms,

Of the 300 rounds of your cartridges fired, none missed fire; some I submerged in water before firing, but they were equally sure, being seemingly water proof. I should always feel sure *my powder was dry* with such amunition.

The firing of the arm at the long range of 1000 yards was very accurate.

The smooth bore with buck and ball cartridge exceed any smooth bore musket for range and accuracy I have ever seen, and must be a truly valuable arm for the army and navy, combining as it does the almost unerring precision of the rifle, with the damaging effects of the buck shot.

The rapidity with which these arms can be loaded and discharged by the rawest soldier *without* the *possibility* of *accident* or mistake gives them great advantages over any arm I have seen. The weight seems to be less than the Springfield regulation arm, which, too, is a great advantage on long marches, and the great advantage of firing with fixed bayonets, the soldier is always ready for bayonet charge.

In conclusion, I must in justice to the great excellence of these arms and your ammunition, say most unqualifiedly that they possess great merit over any other fire arms and amunition I have ever seen 'or tested, and I earnestly hope our government will place them in the hands of every man in the army and navy soon.

Respectfully yours,
J. M. ROBINSON,
Capt. and A. Q. M., U. S. A.

WASHINGTON, D. C., March 18, 1863:

COL. E. G. ALLEN,

National Hotel, Washington, D. C.

SIR : I have examined with care the musket and carbine of your invention, and regard them as a decided improvement on any arm of the kind that I have seen.

I am convinced that it would be wise and economical to supplant all muskets and carbines now in use in our service by these.   Yours truly,

GEO. G. LYON,
Major and A. D. C., Staff of Maj. Gen. Sigel.

105 Hicks Street, Brooklyn, March 27, 1863.
Col. E. G. Allen.

My Dear Sir : It affords me much pleasure to be able to give a favorable answer to your letter of March 20th, 1863, inquiring what opinion I had formed of the Brand breech-loading rifle which you left with me, and also what I thought of your new method of rifling, and of your buck and ball cartridge.

My opinion was favorable to the arm when I first saw it, but so few inventions of the kind stand the test of trial, that I was afraid some serious fault would be developed then which did not appear at first sight. I therefore gave it a thorough test. First as a rifle with your improved twist and form of groove, and afterwards as a smooth-bore shot gun with your compound buck and ball cartridge. After firing 250 rounds with the rifle, with great accuracy, at targets placed from 100 to 5000 feet distance, without any apparent change in the working of the gun, and without leading the barrel a particle, I took out the rifle barrel, and put in its place the smooth-bore, after firing 150 rounds the gun worked as well as when the first cartridge was put in. There was no leakage, neither did a single cartridge fail. I found no trouble in loading in any position, no difficulty in drawing out the cartridge case, and I have never fired an arm that had so little recoil.

In reference to the rifling, I am of the opinion that the form of groove effectually prevents leading the barrel, and have no doubt that the accuracy of the shot was owing, in a great degree, to the form of twist.

My opinion is also favorable as to the buck and ball cartridge. I think the buck-shot used in the ammunition you left with me too small ; but I did not suppose that a round ball could be shot from a smooth-bore gun with such effect. The buck-shot always struck in good line, but the ball penetrated nearly as far as from the rifle, and I was able to send a ball with great accuracy 2000 feet, with but little more elevation than the rifle.

I cannot speak too highly of the buck-and-ball cartridge, containing in one case fulminate, powder, wad, buck-shot, and round ball, and entirely secure from accident or injury.

I consider the arm compact, strong, very simple, not liable to derangement, and altogether a very meritorious invention.

WM. CLEVELAND HICKS,
Civil and Mechanical Engineer.

TREASURY U. S., Oct. 24, 1862.

MY DEAR GENERAL : I have had the satisfaction of examining a breech-loading rifle, invented and in the possession of Colonel Allen, of Massachusetts. There may be a better gun in the world, but although I have made it a point to examine all that I could have access to for many years, I have never seen one that makes any approach to this.

I am so impressed with the great superiority of this gun in almost every essential requisite, that I can't resist urging upon you the necessity of giving it a fair trial, and if found to be what I believe it to be, have you recommend its adoption into the military service of the United States.

Very sincerely yours,
F. E. SPINNER.

MAJ. GEN. JAMES W. RIPLEY,
Chief of Ordnance U. S. A.,
Washington, D. C.

WASHINGTON, March 14, 1863.

COL. E. G. ALLEN.

DEAR SIR : In answer to your inquiries in regard to your breech-loading fire arms and ammunition, I will say that I have tested in every practical mode the metallic cartridge known as E. G. Allen's buck-and-ball cartridge for *smooth-bore fire arms.*

I find the results to be, viz. : That with the *small amount of powder* used the round ball is thrown with *great accuracy* at a short or *long* range, while the *buck*-shot in the cartridge are *very effectual* according to their *size* and *heft.*

In the construction of this cartridge I find fulminating powder in the outer rim, then the charge of powder, and between the powder and buck-shot there is a wad sufficient *to prevent the escape of gas* among the buck-shot, *thus giving* them the *full force of the charge.*

The round shot in the head of the cartridge being a *trifle larger than the bore* of the gun, is *forced* in the barrel when explosion takes place, and the *results* are the same as is *found* in the well-known ball with a patch to prevent the escape of gas, and give it *accuracy* and *force.*

I am familiarly acquainted with all kinds of cartridges in use for smooth-bore guns, and from my large experience with this cartridge I consider it a *very valuable* invention, and of *great importance* to the Government of the United States, as well also for private uses.

In the course of my testing the cartridges at a range of 600 yards, 50 shots were thrown with the *precision* of any target rifle practice I ever witnessed, *striking the small target aimed at in almost every instance.*

These cartridges in transportation are *perfectly safe* from *breakage, or explosion, or dampness*, thus rendering them, *when compared with any other cartridge in use*, valuable on account of their cost.

Respectfully yours,

JOSEPH H. WIGGIN.

OFFICE OF COMMANDANT OF GENERAL HEADQUARTERS.
HEADQUARTERS ARMY OF THE POTOMAC,
Camp near Falmouth, Va., March 14th, 1863.

COL. E. G. ALLEN,

DEAR SIR: Having examined your improved breech-loading fire arms and the cartridges which accompanied them, I take pleasure in acknowledging their merits, as I regard them the most perfect articles of the kind which have yet been presented to the public.

The simplicity of the lock, the groove itself, and the gradual increase of the twist of the groove towards the muzzle, thus increasing the resistance to the flight of the ball, and giving time for the powder to ignite, (by this means rendering a small charge as effective as larger ones in the other rifle muskets,) and actually causing the heat at the point where the powder is discharged to be *less* than at the muzzle, are decided improvements. But your method of avoiding *windage* in shooting buck and ball cartridges from a smooth bore gun is a *valuable* discovery.

These cartridges, as well as your elongated ball cartridges, having the fulminating composition ingeniously disposed within *the cartridges so that the severest tests of handling and throwing them about does not injure nor explode them*, while they in your gun exploded without fail, I regard as a most fortunate and valuable discovery.

The habit of soldiers cleaning the cones of their guns by pol-
ishing or rubbing them so that caps will not stick on them, and
the precious moments lost in action while capping the piece, to
say nothing of the soldier losing his caps in action so that gun
and cartridges are useless, will I trust, soon bring your weapon
into our service and add to our efficiency.

I am Col. very respectfully, your ob't servant,

G. O. HALLER,

Maj. 7th Infantry, Commandant of Gen'l Headquarters.

NATIONAL HOTEL, WASHINGTON, D. C.,

March 11th, 1863.

COL. E. G. ALLEN,

DEAR SIR: I have this day in answer to your request, witnessed and tested the firing of your (Allen & Brand's) rifled musket, carbine, and smooth bore breech-loading fire arms, with your
cartridges for the same.

Three hundred rounds were fired within one hour, in the different arms, and on examination of the different barrels, they
were found to be perfectly in condition for firing again.

There was no *ledding* or *fouling* of the barrels, owing to the peculiar rifling, and the construction of the cartridges, which I
deem an invention of great merit.

The ranges attained were from 200 yards to one mile distant,
at a low elevation. The amount of powder in the cartriges being
less than 44 grains, with the ordinary weight of ball for the arm
known as the Springfield musket. For *range* and *accuracy*, both
were perfect, striking the object aimed at in almost every instance of the firing of 300 rounds.

The arm can be loaded at present arms without endangering
the soldier, by three motions. The recoil is *very* slight in either
of the arms. It has the ordinary Springfield bayonet now in use.

Its weight is less than the Springfield musket, as also are the
cartridges.

These cartridges are water-proof, and not liable to get out of
order when subjected to transportation, and they are perfectly
sure of explosion under any circumstances in the arm. And in
conclusion I will say that I consider either of the arms or amuni-

tion are far superior to any other arm ever placed in my hands, for service or inspection. Its simplicity and apparent durability, *certainty* of closing the breech, and protection against accident, recommends itself to the judgment of any individual who may examine the arm carefully.

Having had several years experience in the United States service, I will say that I consider these *arms* and *amunition* of yours far superior to the arm known as the Springfield musket, or to any arm now in use in the United States service.

I am respectfully, your ob't servant,

WM. BLAISDELL,

Col. com'g 11th Mass. Vol. U. S. A.

HEADQURTERS ARMY OF POTOMAC,

Camp near Falmouth, Va., March 16th, 1863.

COL. E. G. ALLEN, WASHINGTON, D. C.

DEAR SIR: In answer to your inquiry as to my opinion of your breech-loading fire arm, I beg leave to state that having carefully examined and fired it, I consider it the best arm of the kind I have ever seen. Its long *range, trifling recoil, simplicity* of construction, accurate firing and apparent durability, renders it peculiarly well adapted to military use in its various forms.

Your cartridges are *certainly most decided improvements*, certain of fire, (I have never seen one fail,) easy of transportation, and I believe entirely water-proof. They are really a desideratum in the way of amunition.

Very respectfully your obedient servant,

JNO. DICKINSON,

Lieut. Col. and A. A. Gen'l, Army of the Potomac.

ALLEN & BRAND'S BREEOH-LOADING SMOOTH-BORE MUSKET.

NAVY ORDNANCE YARD,
Washington City, Feb. 19, 1863.

CAPTAIN J. A. DAHLGREN,
Chief of Bureau of Ordnance.

SIR : We have examined and tested Allen & Brand's breech-loading smoothe-bore musket, and report as follows :

The arrangements by which it is made a breech-loading arm is identical with that of Brand's patent breech-loading rifled musket, presented by Col. E. G. Allen, of Boston, and examined and reported upon by Lieut. Com. May, June 30, 1862.

Weight of barrel,........................ 3.9 5 lbs.
" of stock,......................... 5.51 "
Weight of gun complete,................. 9.46 "
Weight of regulation, Springfield,.......... 9.14½ lbs.
Length of barrel,........................ 38½ inches.
Calibre,................................. in. 58.

Fixed ammunition was used, which was furnished by the inventor, being metallic, consisting of a cylindrical copper case with fulminate in the rear.

In the cartridges are three buck shot in addition to the bullet, and between the shot and powder is a paper wad.

The following are the mean weights of three cartridges :

Powder,...... 48. 8 grains.
Case,........ 97. 3 "
Ball,........275. 5 "
Buck Shot,.... 75. 9 "
Ward,........ 3. 5 "
────────────
5.01 grains.

Regulation 110 grains for 1 ball, 3 buck-shot and paper cartridges.

Sixty rounds were fired first from the musket for accuracy, and to ascertain how many of the buck-shot (180) would strike a board two feet square placed at fifty yards distant. 58 balls and 32 buck-shot struck.

Forty-seven rounds were then fired from the same musket, 17 of which were fired for penetration at a target two feet square, and made of pine boards 1⅛ inches apart, and 1⅛ inches thick, placed at fifty yards distant.

1 ball passed through 4 boards.
7 " " " 5 "
7 " " " 6 "
1 " " " 7 "
1 went into cleats.
Average penetration, 5½ boards.

At the request of Col. Allen the smooth-bore barrel was then taken off, and a rifle barrel (cal. 54) attached to the stock, and 132 rounds fired from it with cartridges having a conical ball with a solid base.

The following are the mean weights of three cartridges :

Powder,.......... 38. 4 grains.   64 grains regulation.
Case,............. 62. 9   "
Ball,.............473. 4   "
                   ———————
                   574. 7 grains.

Twenty-six of the above were fired for penetration at a similar target placed at 90 yards distant.

Six missed the target.
Three passed through 5 boards.
One " " 6 "
Three " " 8 "
One " " 9 "
Six " " 10 "
Four " " 11 "
Two into cleats.
Average penetration, 12⅜ boards.

———————

{ Springfield musket,
{   8¾ boards.

The balance (106) were fired at random.

During the firing of 50 rounds, the gun heated from 58° to 100 at muzzle, and 70° at breech.

The arm is comparatively light, as will be seen by weights of the parts, the recoil inconsiderable, the lock being in the breech piece *is not apt to work stiff from heating*, and the workmanship of the entire arm is good.

One of the cartridges was submerged in *water 51 hours*, and on examination, the powder found in a perfectly *dry state*.

Respectfully submitted,
(Signed)   WM. MITCHEL, Lieut. Com. U. S. N.
                  JOHN G. MITCHEL, Lieut. Com. U. S. N.

The above corroborates a previous report made last June, by Lieut. Com. May, and on *personal inspection*, the arm has a very *promising appearance.*

J. A. DAHLGREN.

HEAD QUARTERS, ARMY OF THE POTOMAC,
Camp, near Falmouth, March 15, 1863.
SIR : I assisted on the 14th inst. at the experimental practice
with Col. Allen's improved breech-loading gun, and I found it
satisfied all the questions which can be asked for military arms.
First. The long range and accuracy of the ball.
Second. The simplicity of the loading.
Third. Simplicity and durability of the mechanism.
Fourth. The low price at which it can be manufactured.
I have seen many if not all of the modern arms, and I must say
that this gun is the very best of all I have seen.
Very respectfully,
Your obedient servant,
Capt. of the Russian Artillery of Guard.
V. RAYDERISHIN.

WASHINGTON, D. C.
March 19, 1863.
COL. ALLEN : Having had the pleasure this day of examining
minutely the principles and mechanism of your new, beautiful and
effective gun—its convenience, its increase of projectile force, and
its economy of ammunition, I am happy to bear my humble but
earnest testimony to its superior usefulness, and as one officer,
should be glad to see it generally adopted for use in the army.
D. S. CURTISS,
Col. Com. 28th Wis. Vol., U. S. A.

BALTIMORE, Oct. 3, 1862.
HON. MONTGOMERY BLAIR,
U. S. P. M. General, Washington.
DEAR SIR : Permit me to introduce to you Col. E. G. Allen,
who is the inventor of a new breech-loading rifle, which he de-
sires to introduce to the attention of the Government.
He is a gentleman of intelligence. His rifle, in my judgment,
is superior to any other I ever had the pleasure of examining.
I commend him most cordially to your respectful consideration.
Very respectfully your ob't serv't,
HENRY STOCKBRIDGE.

WASHINGTON, D. C., March 23, 1863.

SIR : I have with great pleasure and interest examined your breech-loading system, adapted to smooth-bore and rifled infantry muskets, as well as to rifled carbines for cavalry use, and found it the best improvement I have yet seen.

Among the many advantages your arm possesses over those heretofore brought to my notice, and which in my opinion endow it with peculiar merits, I would mention the following :

The breech or sliding piece to which the cartridge is fastened moves with perfect ease and rapidity.

The small number of parts constituting your system of breech-loading arms, and their simplicity of construction.

The facility and security with which the loading is performed, allowing of the arm being put in the hands of soldiers but imperfectly drilled.

. No perceptible leakage or escape of gas when fired.

The arm cannot be fired without the breech being securely closed.

. No deposit of powder found in the barrel, although fired continually for some time.

Recoil scarcely perceptible, the projectile fired from the arm appearing to describe a very flat trajectory, and to have not only great initial velocity, but also power of penetration exceeding that of the ordinary infantry rifled musket at smaller range.

The employment of cartridges combining in one piece, ball, powder, and priming composition.

The latter I deem of utmost importance, considering the great loss of powder and the *inconvenience* attending the use of ordinary cartridges and caps' particularly in cold and wet weather.

Wishing you all the success that so admirable an invention as the breech-loading arm you submitted to me deserves,

I am, sir, your ob't serv't,

ERNEST VON NEGESACK,

Of the Royal Swedish Army, Col. 20th N. Y. Vols.

HEADQUARTERS ARMY OF THE POTOMAC, ·
Camp near Falmouth, Va.,
March 19, 1863.

COL. E. G. ALLEN, Washington, D. C.

DEAR SIR : In answer to your inquiries in regard to your breech-loading fire arms and ammunition, I will say that I have carefully examined their principles of construction, and tested them by firing.

The arm possesses great merit over every other arm I have seen.

1st. Its simplicity and durability.

2d. Its adaptness as an arm for military service in all its forms.

3d. Its accuracy of firing at long range.

4th. The ammunition possesses great superiority over all other ammunition, especially the buck-and-ball cartridge, which is certainty of explosion when placed in the gun. There can be no damage from transportation, no escape of gas by the shot when · fired.

Their light charges of powder, long range, and accuracy with which the shot are thrown, confirm my opinion of the superiority of the invention.

Respectfully yours,
FRED'K ROSENCRANTZ,
Captain in the Royal Swedish Cavalry.

———

INSPECTOR GENERAL'S DEPARTMENT,
Headquarters Army of the Potomac,
March 15, 1863.

COL. E. G. ALLEN,
Washington, D. C.

DEAR SIR : I have carefully examined your breech-loading rifled musket, " 54 cal.," using a metallic cartridge ; have seen it fired, and fired it myself quite a number of times, and from my examination of and experience with it, I think it the best breech-loadidg arm for troops I have ever seen. Its good proportions, apparent simplicity of structure, and durability ; its range and accuracy of fire, and facility with which it is loaded and discharged, also cleanliness after firing, highly recommend it.

With *good* troops, *well* drilled and disciplined, when properly
used, it would be a most effective weapon. For troops less ex-
perienced in the use of fire arms I should prefer your smooth-
bore musket, " 65 cal.," with buck-and-ball and buck-shot cartridges.

Other things being equal, the dispensing with rammers and
percussion caps in loading, for arms in the hands of troops, as is
the case with your musket, is a most *desirable* end gained for
military service.

Your cartridges, for safety and preservation in transportation,
and use, in point of form and weight, and security against
damage from dampness and wet, meet fully the wants of our
military service.

The want of cartridges less liable to damage than those now
in use, and more easy of access to the soldier on the field of battle than that portion which is placed in the lower magazine of
our cartridge-boxes.

We also want buck-and-ball, and even buck-shot cartridges,
for short ranges and more execution.

Your carbine I judge equal in merit, for the use wanted of it,
to your rifle musket.

For sporting purposes your rifle has high merit, and, with the
shot gun, would prove a most satisfactory arm for the sportsman.

Very respectfully your ob't serv't,
J. H. DAVIS,
Assistant Inspector General U. S. A.

WASHINGTON, D. C., March 18th, 1863.

COL. E. G. ALLEN, WASHINGTON, D. C.

SIR: I have carefully examined your musket and take pleasure in recommending it for the following, among other reasons.

1st. It is well balanced so that good aim can be taken.

2d. It has a long range.

3d. It has all the advantages of any breech-loading gun that
I have seen, and can be loaded in any position, and especially
while lying, without exposure.

4th. It can be loaded and fired with great rapidity, and without fear of heating or putting in several charges.

5th. It is simple in its construction, and hence is easily kept in order and easily repaired.

6th. It is strong and hence will wear long, and cannot easily be injured or destroyed.

7th. Its mechanism adapts its stock to smooth and rifle barrels.

8th. The cartridges can be removed with ease, so that when the men return from picket they can remove them without injury to the barrel or cartridge, and without the waste as in the guns used at present; this is a most important consideration.

9th. The *cartridges* are of good calibre, (58).

10th. They can be transported without danger or waste.

11th. They are perfectly protected from climatic agencies, thus preventing much waste.

12th. They dispense with separate caps, which is an excellent consideration, as *caps* are difficult to handle in cold and wet weather, as they are much wasted, and the want of them is often the only reason for being out of amunition.

13th. The men see their value and relie on them, and hence will not be disposed to waste them either while on the march or in firing.

14th. The *canister* shot for muskets I think of no advantage when small shot are used,

A. As a combat at close quarters, either on the defensive or offensive, should be decided by the bayonet.

B. It is calculated to make the soldier careless of his aim.

C. The small balls have but little effect, and do not instantly disable, and hence they could not drive back a resolute bayonet charge made at close quarters.

15. Buck and ball combined are heavier and make a very desirable amunition.

Very respectfully,

F. SIGEL,
Major Gen'l U. S. A.

P. S. Since writing the above I have seen your rifle, smooth bore and carbine tried, and am free to say that they surpass my expectations. The range is long and accurate, the barrels are changed quickly, the firing rapid, and the ball strikes with great effect.

F. SIGEL,
Major Gen'l U. S. A.

Headquarters, Department of Washington,

March 23d, 1863.

Col. E. G. Allen.

Dear Sir: In compliance with your request for my opinion on your breech-loading fire arms and ammunition, it gives me pleasure to say that I have given them careful examination and test.

Both the arms and ammunition possess great merit over any I have seen.

1st. Their simplicity, strength, and durability.

2d. Their great accuracy, penetration, and long range.

3d. Their almost entire freedom from recoil.

4th. Their being *lighter* than the *regulation musket.*

5th. That they *do not heat at the lock works* from continued and rapid firing.

6th. That they can be loaded and fired in any position without exposing the soldier, which is a very great consideration.

7th. That they *never* lead and do not foul " as do other arms," owing to their peculiar construction, and *the admirable cartridge* used.

In conclusion, I will say that I should be glad to see your breech-loading arms in the hands of our troops, as they possess advantages over any other arm in use, for the *extermination of domestic traitors* or foreign foes.

Very respectfully, your most ob't servant,

DRAKE DeKAY,

A. A. Gen'l, U. S. A.

Washington Arsenal,

Feb. 26, 1863.

Sir: We, the undersigned, have the honor to report that we have examined and tried Mr. E. G. Allen's ammunition for his breech-loading smooth-bore and rifled arms.

These cartridges are made of copper, the form of the ordinary copper cartridges. That for the smooth-bore, having a round ball and three buck-shot, a wad being between the buck and powder.

The following are the weights as ascertained.

3

Smooth-bore   Cartridge,

Weight of powder,.... 44 grains.
"   " round ball,..283⅜ "
"   " 3 buck-shot,. 75   "
"   " wad,........ 4   "
"   " case,........ 94⅓ "

Total,............ 501 grains.

Rifle Cartridge.

"   " powder,.... 38 2–10 gs.
"   " ball,.······ 474   "
"   " case,...... 62 4–10 "

Total,........ 574 7–10 grains.

The trials of the above ammunition were made with the same stock and breech piece, and with three different barrels, a smooth-bore rifle and carbine, all cal. 58. The breech-piece of the arm for which this ammunition is intended, is opened and closed by means of a lever on top of the neck of the stock. This lever is composed of two toggle joints, working in the form of a truss. There is a clutch on the end of the breech-piece next the barrel, that holds and carries the cartridge in a direct line with the barrel when the gun is being loaded, and removes the case when opened. The trigger is stationary while the lock and sear that operates upon the hammer are moveable, and are so arranged that the gun cannot be fired when the breech is open, and when it is partially closed the cocking of the gun closes it firmly.

The rifling of the rifle is an irregular gain twist, being nearly straight at the breech for several inches, then increasing slowly till near the muzzle, where it increases very rapidly, being at the muzzle one turn in 28 inches.

The cartridge presented for trial in the smooth-bore gun was (as above described) the usual metal case revolving round a ball, and three buck-shot. The diameter of the ball being greater than that of the muzzle of the gun The following are the results of the trial of this cartridge :

Average penetration, 7 inches.
Range, excellent.
Accuracy, great.

The buck-shot used are too light, and could not be effective except at very close quarters. At thirty yards they will not penetrate or bury themselves in a pine board one inch thick.

Next, as regards the trial of the carbine ammunition, the average penetration was nine inches. Its range very great, (and especially so when the small amount of powder used is considered) its accuracy unvarying.

Of Mr. Allen's rifle, nothing can be said which may not be said of the carbine. The recoil of any of these arms is very slight. Both the arm and ammunition possesses unqualified merit.

Respectfully submitted,

(Signed,)   J. C. BRADFORD, 1st Lt. Ord.

L. S. BABBITT, 2d Lt.

To Lieutenant Col. Geo. D. Ramsay, U. S. Ord.,

Com. Washington Arsenal.

[Official copy.]   J. G. BENTON, Capt.

ORDNANCE OFFICE, ARMY OF POTOMAC,
March 14, 1863.

COL. E. G. ALLEN.

WASHINGTON, D. C.

SIR : In answer to your communication I have to state that I have examined the ammunition of your breech-loading rifle, and also the rifle itself.

I saw the rifle and fired it several times myself. The range at which it was fired was two hundred yards, the recoil was very slight. It can be loaded and fired with ease and great rapidity, and its fire is accurate. We had no means of estimating the penetration.

Both the *rifle* and *ammunition* possess many merits and I can find no fault with it.

It is very servicable, not too heavy, and in my opinion well adapted to the use of troops.

I am Col., very respectfully, your ob't servant,

D. W. HAGLER,

Chief Ordnance Officer, Army of Potomac.

U. S. Navy Yard,
New York, March 30, 1863.

Dear Sir : Your letter, asking my opinion of your buck and ball cartridge, was duly received.

In my official report to the Chief of the Bureau of Ordnance, I believe I stated all that I knew of it from the limited experiments with it. I may have omitted to speak of its qualities as a manufactured article, in fact, I did make this omission. This was not intended, for I made experiments particularly with a view to try them in this respect, and to make mention of results.

The trial, as you will remember, was with four different kinds of cartridges made for fixed ammunition. Ten of each kind were dropped from the height of my shoulder, (about 4 ft. 6 in.) on to the stone floor of an ordnance office, and no one of them stood more than two droppings. You then *threw yours* up to the wall overhead, (about 12 feet,) letting them fall to the same. They were uninjured.

As to the certainty of explosion, there can be no doubt on the subject. Of their water-proof qualities, no one can doubt, when any of them was soaked for 54 hours, and the powder in it at the end of that time, was perfectly dry. This was not a sample cartridge, but one which you had been carrying loose in your pocket.

Besides all this, I might perhaps, say that the arm you use and the cartridge going with it, made the happiest combination I have ever seen.

The charge of powder used is much less than in our government arm, while the penetration is quite equal to it.

The arm heats but little at the breech, which prevents any swelling of the working parts and the consequence attending.— I am only sorry I could not have had a more varied trial of the piece, as I should then, perhaps, have been able to give facts, while now I am obliged to give opinions, only, from the few experiments. Wishing you all possible success,

I remain, yours truly,
JOHN A. MITCHEL,
Lieut. Com. U. S. N.

Col. E. G. Allen,
National Hotel, Washington, D. C.

HEADQUARTERS BRIGADE, 1ST CAVALRY DIVISION,
Camp near Stafford, March 31, 1863.

COLONEL.

In reply to your request for my opinion on your Breech-Loading Fire Arms and Ammunition, I am happy to state that, in so far as their adaptability to the Cavalry Arm of the service is concerned, they are the best I have ever examined.

Their simplicity and strength of construction, the readiness with which they can be loaded in any position on horseback, their unusual length of range, the facility with which the ammunition can be used, the safety with which it can be carried and transported, and the certainty that it can always be depended upon in any weather, combined to render this arm and its ammunition peculiarly suited for mounted service ; and I earnestly trust that its use will be adopted, and your invention receive the encouragement it undoubtedly deserves.

Very respectfully, your obedient servant,
THOS. C. DEVINS,
Colonel, 6th N. Y. Vol., Cavalry,
Com. 2d Brigade Cav. Camp.

COL. E. G. ALLEN,
Washington, D. C.

———

Head-Quarters Army of the Potomac,
April 6th, 1863.

COL. ALLEN.

COLONEL :—I have witnessed a test of your breech-loading musket and carbine with much satisfaction.

For rapidity and precison of firing, I have never seen it excelled.

The metallic cartridges, although originally costing more than the paper, will, I think, from their indestructability, be a great saving if adopted in the service.

The gun is very light, and indeed, I have no fault to find with it. I have no doubt it will soon be generally adopted.

Very respectfully, your obedient servant,
H. W. PERKINS,
Lieut. and A. D. C.

New York, April 19th, 1863.

Col. E. G. Allen.

Dear Sir :—Please to manufacture for my private use, a "Sporting Target Rifle," 28 in. barrel ; also, "Shot Barrel." I desire the ball of rifle to be ½ oz. accompanying the gun, with sufficient cartridges, say 300 of each. I desire the Allen & Brand's patents. You will ship to me by the United States Express, to Denver City, Colorado Territory, marked, C. O. D.

After an experience of several years in the Rocky Mountains, and in a search for the best weapons in use, I have selected yours as the most perfect. I have used all of the late patents of guns, including the Maynard, but regard yours as infinitely better than the best in use. Your improved cartridge is so reliable and cheap, combined with safety, that to any one who requires the use of arms, they seem indispensible.

Yours very respectfully,

HON. JOS. KENYON,

Denver City, Colorado Ter.

Head-Quarters Army of the Potomac.
April 4th, 1863.

Col. E. G. Allen.

National Hotel, Washington.

Colonel :—I take great pleasure in adding my testimony to the many already in your possession, as to the accuracy and general efficiency of your breech-loading gun. I have carefully examined and tested it with the conical ball, and found it to shoot with remarkable accuracy and hardly preceptible recoil.

It combines the advantages of the rifled arm with those of a breech-loading and percussion cartridge, and from the peculiarity of its rifling, more accuracy than the ordinary Springfield rifled musket.

In conclusion, I consider it by far the most effective weapon I have seen, for the use of infantry or cavalry.

Very respectfully, your obedient servant,

WM. L. CANDLER,

Capt. and A. D. C. to Maj.-Gen. Hooker.

Head-Quarters 20th Regt. Maine Vols.,
3d Brigade, 1st Division, 5th Army Corps,
Army of the Potomac, near Falmouth,
April 7th, 1863.

COL. E. G. ALLEN.

DEAR SIR:—Having seen your breech-loading arm tested at various ranges to-day, and having carefully examined it, I must say, (although previously prejudiced against breech-loading arms,) that I consider this the *very best arm* for field service I have ever seen.

If our infantry regiments could be armed with this arm, (the flank companies with the rifle and the others with the smooth bore for buck and ball,) I really think we should have the most effective army the world ever saw.

Your obedient servant,

CHAS. L. GILMORE,

Major 30th Regt., Maine Vol.

Head-Quarters Army of the Potomac,
March 14th, 1863.

COL. E. G. ALLEN.

National Hotel, Washington.

COLONEL:—I wish to express to you the great satisfaction I felt last week, on testing your admirable breech-loading musket and carbine.

For accuracy and efficiency as a military arm, I have no hesitation in saying I consider it without an equal, and most admirably adapted for the use of light troops.

Very respectfully, your obedient servant,
HENRY RUSSELL,
Capt. and A. D. C. to Maj.-Gen. Hooker.

Head-Quarters 3d Army Corps
April 3d, 1863.

Col. E. G. Allen,

Having been invited to examine and test your new breech-loading rifle and smooth bore gun, and report the results, I have to say that in construction, it is the most simple and compact of any fire arm I have ever seen. It can be loaded by the soldier in almost any position without exposing his arms unnecessarily to the enemies' shot.

The formation of the cartridges is such as to be easily and securely handled—a most important desideratum in wet and cold weather. The piece is lighter than the arms now in use.

I tested the smooth bore, distance 250 yds., point blank, off hand shots ; the target, a quarter of a sheet of common sized writing paper, was perforated at nearly every shot, and every shot being in perfect line. The rifle at same distance, off hand, was a sure shot, and at the distance of 1,000 yds., off hand, 3 or 5 shots perforated the target, (white paper, 12 in. square.)

I fired at same time, the Springfield Minie musket and Sharp's rifle, and their shooting is not to be compared. with that of your gun. The recoil of either being much greater than that of yours, which is a great point in the mind of the soldier, and it is impossible for two loads to be in the barrel at one time ; a very important matter, when viewed with reference to scenes on the battlefield, where our country needs every gun in perfect working order. In a word, it is my opinion it is the most effective fire arm that can be placed in the hands of a soldier, and if there is such a thing as a substitute for discipline in old or new troops in the field of battle, it is your bayonet rifle.

DAVID A. GRANGER,
1st Lieut., Comd'g Provost Guard.—3d Army Corps

Head-Quarters 6th Maine Battery,
2d Division, 12th Corps d' Armee,
Dumfries, Va., April 7th, 1863.

Col. E. G. Allen.

Dear Sir :—In reply to your request for my opinion on your breech-loading fire arms and ammunition, it gives me great pleasure to state that, after a thorough test and careful examination of these arms and ammunition, I unreservedly pronounce them the best I have ever seen.

1st.—The various arms are all equally strong and simple.

2d.—Their strength and simplicity give them every advantage over any arms now in use.

3d.—They are lighter than any arms now in use.

4th.—Their penetration is great at long range.

5th.—They throw a ball with great precision.

6th.—They have the very great advantage of being loaded and fired in any position, without exposing the soldier.

7th.—They never become heated about the lock works from long firing.

8th.—They do not lead, owing to their peculiar grooving.

Finally, they are simple, strong, durable, and not liable to get out of order in the hands of undrilled troops.

The ammunition is superior to any I have ever seen ; they will stand any rough usage in handling and transportation, and are water-proof. The soldier can always rely upon every cartridge, thus making them economical to the government, there being no loss by breakage in transporting them.

In the common cartridge box for the Springfield musket, which contains forty rounds of ammunition, eighty-four rounds of this ammunition occupy the same space.

In regard to the cartridge for smooth bores, being composed of from three to nine buck shot, one round ball, wad between the powder and shot, powder and fulminate, all combined in one metallic case and water-proof, I consider a *valuable invention of great importance* for field service or private use, and trust that the ammunition and arms may be adopted for general use in the army, &c.

I am, Colonel, very respectfully,
Your obedient servant,
EDWIN B. DOW,
Lieut. Com'dg. 6th Maine Battery.

Head-Quarters Army of the Potomac,
April 7th, 1863.

Requisition for Ordnance and Ordnance Stores for the use of the 11th Massachusetts Volunteer Regiment, commanded by Col. Wm. Blaisdell.

No. to be supplied.

111 Rifled muskets—breech loading—Allen & Brand's
     Patent; and regulation Springfield bayonets.
30,000 Cartridges, fixed ammunition. Cal. 54, to suit
     the arms.
111 Cartridge Boxes,
111 Cartridge Box Belts, } to suit the arms required.
111 Waist Belts,
111 Bayonet Scabbards,

I certify that the above order is correct, and that it is absotely necessary that the arms should be furnished.

WILLIAM BLAISDELL,
Col. Com'd Regiment.

The above requisition is approved by me, and immediate issue is necessary.

JOS. B. CARR,
Comd'g Brigade.

Approved, D. E. SICKLES,
Maj.-Gen'l Commanding.

Approved, JOSEPH HOOKER,
Maj.-Gen'l Commanding.

———

Head-Quarters 20th Maine Volunteers.
Camp near Falmouth, Va.,
April 8th, 1863.

COL. E. G. ALLEN.

COLONEL :—We have examined your breech-loading rifle and witnessed the target practice with it, and take great pleasure in expressing our high opinion of its qualities.

It seems to fulfill all the requsites to arm, thoroughly, troops for the field. The simplicity and compactness of the piece, its strength and evident durability, its freedom from liability to injury by the ordinary usage in the hands of soldiers and from accidental discharge, render it far superior to any arm now in use. The rifling, by its irregular increase of twist, causing the motion of the ball to be given gradually and to reach its maximum at the muzzle, enables the powder to act with full force, and also gives a steadiness of flight that is not otherwise obtained.—As an arm for mounted troops, we think your carbine cannot be surpassed.

The cartridge is complete of itself, and so adjusted in loading, as to permit no escape of gas at the breech, and to retain the full force of the charge.

With the buck and ball cartridges, prepared in the way they are, the smooth bore possesses all the advantages of a rifle.

The facility of loading is remarkable : any exposure of the person is avoided, not of skirmishers only, but of troops in position behind cover of any kind, and thus gives a great superiority over guns loaded by use of rammer.

The practice, as seen by us, was excellent. We believe the efficiency of our army would be greatly enhanced by the adoption of this arm.

We are, sir, most respectfully,

Your obedient servants,

A. AMES,

Col. 20th, Regiment, Maine Vols,

J. S. CHAMBERLAIN,

Lieut.-Col. 20th Regt., Maine Vols.

———

WASHINGTON, D. C., April 10th, 1863.

MR. E. G. ALLEN,

National Hotel,

SIR—Having witnessed the firing with your breech-loading rifle, at the camp of the 20th Me. Reg't, in accordance with instructions received from Major-Gen. Geo. D. Mead, comd'g 4th Corps, I hereby cheerfully indorse the views expressed in the letter of Col. A. Ames in regard to its accuracy as a rifle or smooth-bore, and its simplicity as a breech-loader.

The breech and reinforce, I found to remain cool, although the chase and muzzle were too hot to hold in the hand. The recoil was slight and did not increase apparently.

The firing with the rifle barrel was accurate, and with the smooth-bore with buck and ball most satisfactory.

After a thorough examination, I would gladly recommend the putting of a number of these guns in the hands of troops in the field, the only practical test, feeling confident that they will stand the rough handling and the severe test to what they will be put.

I remain, your obd't serv't,

ALEX. S. WEBB,

Lt. Col. Asst. Inspt. Gen. 5th Army Corps,

By order of Capt. U. S. Army.

Maj-Gen. MEAD,

Comd'g 5th Army Corps.

Head-Quarters 3d Army Corps,

April 7th, 1863.

COL. E. G. ALLEN,

DEAR SIR : Having tested the qualities of your breech-loading arm, and the principle of the ammunition exhibited by you. It affords me a great degree of satisfaction to certify that, I regard the arm as the best in the service for accuracy at long range. In simplicity, durability, and practicability, it *has no superior.*

With particular reference to the ammunition, I believe it much cheaper than the ordinary ammunition used in the American service, as there is no waste from exposure or dampness.

I am, Col. very respectfully your obd't serv't,

O. H. HART,

Lt. Col. and Asst. Adj't Gen.

By command of 3d Army Corps.

Maj.-Gen. D. E. SICKLES.

West Point, N. Y., April 23d, 1863.

Col. E. G. Allen, New York.

Sir :—I take pleasure in giving you my opinion of the performance of your breech-loading small arms, tried by you this morning. A rifle of the same patent was familiar to me, but the arms presented to-day seemed an improvement.

The smooth bore carrying a ball and buck shot cartridge *gave excellent results*, throwing the buck shot to 100—150 yards, and the ball with very considerable accuracy up to 500 yards and over.

This was fired over 100 rounds without difficulty—the barrel was found very much heated at the muzzle, but *but very slightly at the breech*, where indeed it was *comparatively cool*.

The carbine, 22 in. barrel, using the rifle ammunition, gave most favorable results. It fired with *remarkable accuracy, to the distance of* 700 *yards*, and carried its projectile at proper elevation over 1000 yards. I noticed no difference between the performance of the short carbine and the rifle with ordinary length of barrel, except that the recoil of the former, although not severe is much greater than of the latter. The use of the same weight, powder and shot, with so light a weapon, accounts for this difference.

No target practice was made, but over 250 rounds were fired from the guns in the space of 1½ hours, and the general results were as follows :

1st.—The *great range* and *projectile force attained with so* light a charge of powder.

2d.—The general accuracy of fire.

3d.—The *very slight recoil*.

4th.—The *very slight heating* of the breech and its surroundings.

5th.—In the case of the smooth bore, the superior excellence of its fire *over the ordinary muzzle* loading smooth bore.

6th.—*The easy, sure and safe working* of the breech arrangement

The arms performed to my great satisfaction, and there is no doubt in my mind of their *superior merit*.

Very respectfully, your obd't serv't,

S. V. BENET,

Capt. Ordnance.

ERRATA.

Ernest Von Negersack, p. 29, should read ERNEST VON VEGERSACK.

Jno. Dickinson, on page 25, should read Jos. DICKERSON.

T. V. Benet, on page 17, should read S. V. BENET.

The Merrill Carbine, *Loaded, Cocked and Ready for Firing.*

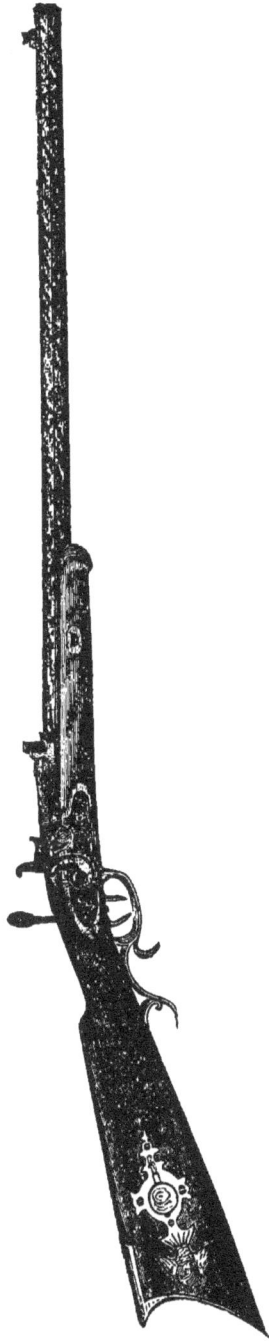

The Merrill Sporting Rifle, *with Globe Sight.*

The Merrill Rifle, *in Position to Receive the Cartridge.*

EHLERS. S.C.

32

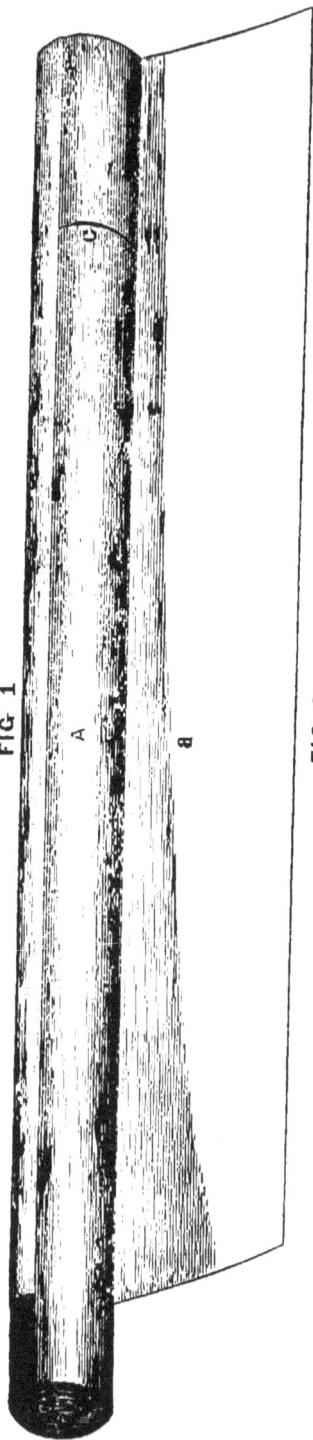

The Merrill Rifle, *Showing the Manner of Making Cartridges.*

FIG 1

FIG 2

FIG 3

FIG 4

Fig. 1.

A — Cartridge Stick.
B — Paper in Process of being Rolled around Cartridge Stick, to be formed into a Tube, as in Fig. 2.
C — Groove to Gauge Length to Cut off Cartridge.

Fig. 2.

A — Cartridge Stick.
B — Paper Pasted into a Tube around Stick.
C — Dotted Line, indicating where to cut off Cartridge at Groove C, in Fig. 1.
D — Cartridge Case, with Ball Pasted or Tied on.

Fig. 3.—Conical Ball.

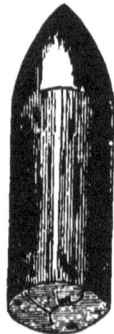

Fig. 4.—Completed Cartridge, Filled and Ready for Use, the End being Turned Over and Pasted Down.

DIRECTIONS

Making Merrill's Cartridges,

AS ILLUSTRATED ON PRECEDING PAGE.

———————◆———————

CUT a piece of paper, nearly the length of Cartridge Stick, as shewn in Fig. 1, and sufficiently wide to allow of its being lapped over and pasted, which, when done, draw the paper off, and when the paste is dry, replace the paper on the stick, letting it project beyond the stick the distance the ball requires for pasting to the paper. Paste the ball to the paper, and by rolling the pasted part with the hand on a table, the ball will adhere to the paper. Then cut the paper around, as shown by dotted line, C, in Fig. 2, and slip the Cartridge Case off the stick with the ball attached. When dry, fill with powder, allowing sufficient paper to turn over, and paste down, as shown in Fig. 4. The Cartridge is then made. Before using, the ball should be well greased with a coat of tallow, put on with a brush while the tallow is melted.

The best paste is made of Gum Shellac, or Gum Arabic.

34

The Merrill Rifle, *Showing Position for Loading or Cleaning.*

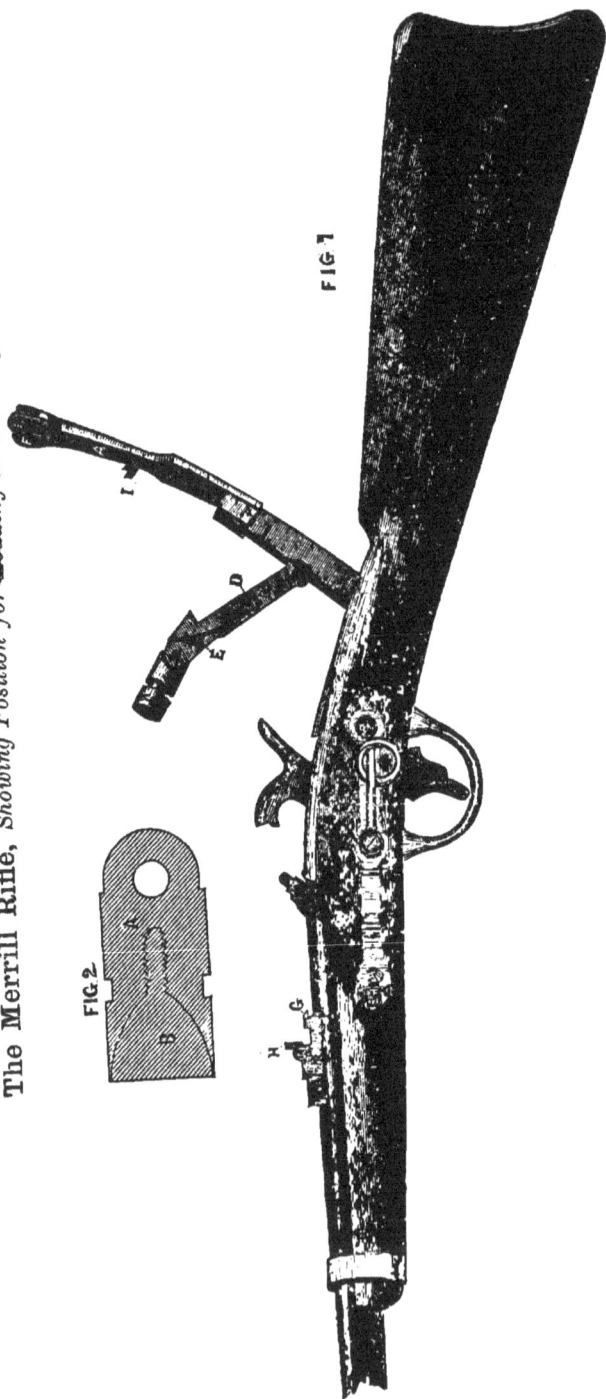

FIG 2

FIG 1

Fig. 1, Showing Link and Plunger out for Cleaning.
A — Lever.
B — Link.
C — Plunger.
D — Guide Screw Track.
E — Guide Screw Switch-off.
F — Lever Spring Bolt.

G — Lever Spring Catch.
H — Elevating Three Leaf Sight.
I — Projection on Lever for Removing Exploded Cap, in raising Lever to Reload.

Fig. 2, Showing Sectional View of Plunger.
A — Plunger.
B — Conical Copper Plug Screwed into Plunger.

Directions for Loading and Cleaning.

TO LOAD WITH CARTRIDGES.

RAISE the hammer to cock or half-cock, draw back the spring catch on end of lever, and raise lever at same time to full height; insert the cartridge without breaking it, and shut the lever down; cap, and the arm is ready for firing. The lever, in being raised after the shot has been fired, removes the exploded cap from the nipple.

TO LOAD WITH LOOSE POWDER AND BALL.

Cock and raise the lever as above, hold the muzzle of the barrel down, drop in a ball, and close the lever, which puts the ball forward to its place. Raise the lever again, and pour the powder from the flask in behind the ball; shut the lever down, and with the exception of capping, the arm is ready for firing.

DIRECTIONS FOR CLEANING.

Raise the lever, and wipe the barrel out with a greased rag, fastened on the end of the cleaning rod, and by looking through the barrel from the muzzle, it can be seen when the barrel is clean. Press the left thumb under the link when the lever is at full height, and keeping the thumb in that position, shut the lever down slowly, which will cause the guide-screw to switch off the track, allowing the link and plunger to come out, which wipe with an oiled rag, and return to their place, by putting the point of the guide-screw in the "switch-off," and raising the lever to full height, which puts the guide-screw on the track again. Then wipe all the iron work with an oiled rag, when the arm can be put away, and will be in good order when wanted.

Any number of shots can be fired without cleaning, but this, like any other gun, should not be put away without being cleaned and oiled.

The balls should always be greased, as no patch is used. The best way to do this is to melt one-third of bees-wax to two-thirds of tallow together, stir until well mixed, and dip the balls in while the tallow is warm; take them out as soon as possible, and a sufficient quantity will remain on the ball for lubrication.

THE
Merrill Patent Breech-Loading Rifle.

———————•———————

THE MERRILL PATENT FIRE ARM MANUFACTURING COMPANY, in offering their Arms to the Public, take this means of informing those not acquainted with the Arms of their Manufacture, that the MERRILL RIFLE is the result of a great deal of experiment by the Inventor, "Mr. JAMES H. MERRILL, of Baltimore," whose vast experience and long practical study in the manufacture of Arms, both in America and Europe, has enabled him to give to the world this great improvement in small arms, which classes him among the most prominent of modern inventors.

The simplicity and strength of construction arrived at in the Merrill Rifle is only equalled by its extraordinary range and accuracy of fire, and the efficiency of the arm not being dependant on any patent *metalic* or *india rubber* cartridge case, but using the simple paper cartridge, or loose powder and ball, and the ordinary percussion cap, (to be had at any country store or trading station,) gives them great advantages over arms depending on fixed or regularly prepared ammunition, and makes them justly preferred, not only on the frontier, but wherever a Rifle is required. Having been approved of by the United States' Government, after being subjected to the most severe tests by both the Army and Navy Departments, and both having ordered them for service, it is with entire confidence they are offered to the Public.

Another advantage the Merrill Plan possesses is, that it can be easily applied to muzzle loading arms at a small cost, without restocking, altering the lock, or changing the general appearance, or diminishing the strength of the arm. The alteration of Muzzle-Loaders to the Merrill Plan of Breech-Loading, has been practically tested by the United States Government with the most entire success, and has placed in the hands of the troops an arm that cannot be surpassed, and also at a small cost.

A great advantage is claimed for these Arms, in being solid in their construction. Like the Regulation Muzzle-Loading Arms, the sabre or ordinary bayonet can be used on them, whereas the Breech-Loading Arms, in which the barrels move, cannot stand the shock of a charge, and are awkward to use when their length is increased by the bayonet. The addition in length to the Merrill Rifle makes no difference in handling it with as much ease as without the bayonet.

For sporting purposes or target shooting, it cannot be equaled, as it has attained the highest perfection in every respect. The barrels are of the best material, and the chambers are bored out to the exact size of the conical ball which they use, so that the plunger which puts the cartridge in its place forces the point of the ball firmly into the grooves or rifling of the barrel, thereby ensuring its going straight to the mark, and not turning, as conical balls frequently do when fired from other rifles.

The Sporting Rifles are fitted with globe sights of the most approved pattern, which ensures fine shooting. These Rifles have been fired *five hundred times* without cleaning, and *any number* of shots can be discharged without any change taking place in the working of the machinery. This is owing to there being no escape of gas, which, when escaping, causes what has been termed *clogging*, in other breech-loaders, but which can never occur with the Merrill Rifle, as the plunger or breech-pin is reamed out so as to make an expansive spring, and the cavity being filled up with copper, upon which the force and heat of the explosion acts at the moment of discharge, causes the plunger to expand as much as the barrel will allow it, or, in other words, to keep up with the expansion of the barrel or surrounding surfaces, and thereby prevent escape of gas, which not only clogs up the working parts of a gun when escaping, but causes great loss of power. Thus no gas escaping from the Merrill Rifle, accounts for its having more penetration than other Breech-Loaders. Attention is respectfully called to the recommendations on the following pages, and any further information will be given, on application by mail, or in person, to

THE MERRILL
PATENT FIRE ARM
MANUFACTURING CO.,
BALTIMORE, MD.

Extract from Lieut. F. K. MURRAY's *U. S. N. Report.*

ORDNANCE OFFICE, U. S. NAVY YARD.
WASHINGTON, *October* 28, 1858.

CAPTAIN INGRAHAM,
Chief of Bureau of Ordnance and Hydrography.

SIR:

In obedience to your order, I have again tested Merrill's plain for altering the Jenks Carbine.

On the 20th instant Mr. Merrill presented himself with two carbines, furnished some time since from the Department, altered as described in my report of June 30th, and differing from each other only in the mode of detaching the upron from the catch upon the barrel; one requiring a forward, the other a backward movement of the springs—the latter mode I prefer. Two kinds of

4

cartridges accompanied these arms; of each the cylindrical part was grooved and perforated, one conically, the other cylindrically. They were coated with bees-wax and tallow. On the 20th instant, I caused one hundred and twenty-six rounds to be fired from one of the carbines, and thirty from the other, at the rate of a little less than four shots per minute, with occasional interruptions caused by vessels passing.

They were then thoroughly sprinkled with water and set aside.

On the 21st, that from which the greater number of rounds had been fired, was again discharged twenty times. Loaded with cartridge, immersed nearly to the muzzle for sixty seconds in water, and again set aside.

On the 22nd, twenty-four hours having elapsed, the carbine was discharged, and, though much rusted, I found no difficulty in firing fifty rounds from it with the usual rapidity, at the close of which the working parts moved freely and smoothly as at the commencement of the trial upon the 20th, being well lubricated by the oil from the cartridge.

In testing for penetration, I found that the ball with the conical cavity gave the best results, passed through seven inches of pine boards at fifty yards. But the form of the ball, number and depth of grooves of rifle, &c. will, I presume, be matters for future decision by the Bureau, should it decide to adopt Mr. Merrill's plan.

The results of the last trial of it, confirm the favorable opinion I expressed in relation to the first, in my report of the 30th June.

I have the honor to be,

Very respectfully,

(Signed)   F. K. MURRAY, *Executive Officer,*
Ordnance Department.

Extract from Report of July 6th.

NAVY YARD, WASHINGTON, *July 6th,* 1859.

Bureau of Ordnance and Hydrography,
    July 7th, 1859.

    Forwarded by

(Signed)   D. N. INGRAHAM,
    Chief of the Bureau.

SIR;

In obedience to your order of the 23rd ult., the undersigned appointed thereby a Board to test the comparative merits of various small arms, especially as to their adaptation to the Naval Service, have tested Merrill's Breech-Loading Apparatus, attached to one of the Plymouth's muskets, which was fired five hundred times at a target, distant five hundred yards. To the merits of these several designs the attention of the Board was directed, in order to determine the facility, security, and endurance of each of these different modes. The above-mentioned arms stood the tests applied to them without material impediment to their continued use, the Board therefore recommends that they may be subjected to the test of service afloat, in such proportions as may be deemed advisable by the Department, to secure the only reliable evidence of their real and comparative merits. In making this recommendation, the Board deem it proper to remark, that the arms differ in calibre and other important details, and therefore if introduced into the service, should be required to conform to the standard of the service as to calibre, weight, and general description of piece, which has since been done, otherwise great confusion would arise, particularly where bodies of seamen were brought together for any particular object.

We have the honor to be,

Very respectfully,

Your obedient Servants,

(Signed)   ANDW. A. HARWOOD, *Captain, U. S. N.*

"   JNO. A. DAHLGREN, *Com., U. S. N.*

"   WM. L. MAURY, *Lieut., U. S. N.*

To the Honorable
ISAAC TOUCEY,
Secretary of the Navy.

Extract from a Letter from A. C. GILLEM, 1st *Lieutenant,* 1st *Artillery, U. S. Army.*

FORT BROWN, TEXAS, *August 9th,* 1860.

MY DEAR SIR:

*　*　*　*　*　*　*　*　*　*　*　*　*　*

Now as to the Gun, or rather Rifle, it has been my constant companion for nearly two years. I have used it in all seasons, and in all kinds of weather; in fact, I have never marched without it, and during that time it has never failed, either firing or in the mechanism. I can fire it five times to any man's four, with Sharp's, and I find it very easy to make the cartridges. Have any of them been ordered by the Department? get the Secretary to order fifty, and I think the report of any Cavalry Officer would be favorable. I prefer them infinitely to Sharp's; neither of mine, Carbine or Rifle, have ever been out of order. I only wish I had brought out a Sporting Rifle of about sixty balls to the pound, (round ball weight.) I shall be happy to hear from you, and of your success.

Yours sincerely,

(Signed)   A. C. GILLEM.

JAS. H. MERRILL, Esq.

6

Letter from S. ADAMS, Esq., *Master Armorer, Va. State Armory.*

SPRINGFIELD, MASS., *Dec.* 25, 1860.

MERRILL'S PATENT FIRE ARM MANUFACTURING CO. :

I wrote a long letter to the Commissioners yesterday, recommending your Breech-Loading Carbine to their *special attention.* The more I deliberate on the simple arrangement of the Breech-Loading principle of your Gun, the more I am persuaded to believe, that it is one of the best Breech-Loading Arms now in use; and on further examination, should your Carbine continue to sustain its already well-earned reputation, I shall have no hesitation in recommending it as the *best Breech-Loading* arm for Cavalry service now made.

Yours with great respect,

(Signed)   S. ADAMS, *M. Armorer,*
State Armory.

———

Extract from Report of Major R. E. COLSTON, *Virginia Military Institute, to the Commissioners on the Virginia Armory—Submitted June* 28, 1860.

WITH REGARD TO CAVALRY. —The experience of armies show that they must be furnished with carbines. But one of the obstacles in the way of using these arms has been the extreme difficulty of loading quickly on horseback, by using a ramrod. I think it indispensable, to place cavalry on a proper footing of efficiency, that they should be supplied with breech-loading carbines. The objections which oppose the introduction of such arms in the infantry, do not apply to cavalry. The strength of the latter is in their shock. The spur and the sabre is what the horseman should depend upon. He will not therefore be tempted to waste his stock of ammunition in useless firing. He will use his carbine only when on outpost service or a skirmisher. In some very rare circumstances, cavalry dismounted have been able to defend a defile or a post by their fire. Breech-loading carbines are now made which shoot with great force and accuracy up to 800 yards. Some arm of this sort should be selected.

Having expressed these general ideas, I pass on to a more particular discussion of the different arms which I have tried.

SMITH & POULTNEY'S CARBINE.—This arm loads with facility while clean, but as I stated before, 60 consecutive shots clogged it up so that it could no longer be worked. This gun was not exposed to the weather nor to any rough usage. From the little rust which has formed upon it, together with the foulness resulting from firing, it is now unfit for service until thoroughly cleaned. But should it not have clogged as it did, I would still consider it as unfit for military service. As the objections which apply to it extend to other arms also, I will state them fully.

The first is *the cost.* I do not think that the state of Virginia, out of the limited appropriation made for the purchase of arms, can afford to buy arms at such a high price. The objection applies to Burnside's and Maynard's gun.

The second and principal objection is *the cartridge.* This is made of india rubber. It is impossible to use the gun without it. It is represented that the cartridge case is susceptible of being used some twenty times, provided it be not lost. I would submit the following considerations:

A sportman in the field shooting partridges or other game, would in no very long time lose many if not all of such cartridges; for in the excitement incident to the sport, he would think it less important to save an empty cartridge case than to get another shot quickly. If this be so, how can it be supposed that the soldier in action, with the enemy before him, is going to put away carefully an empty case, especially on horseback. It would be almost an impossibility to teach regular soldiers to do it. How much more difficult with volunteers or militia? If such arms were purchased and put in the hands of our state troops, with a supply of ammunition, this ammunition would be spent in target or other shooting—and it is almost certain that at the end of a few months the cartridge cases would have disappeared. If the troops were called out on active service, the waste would be still greater. The supply of ammunition would depend upon machinery; and should the troops be furnished with the guns, the powder and the lead, unless they had the cartridge cases, the arms would be useless. It is most probable that these cases would not be used on an average more than twice; which would render them very expensive. I consider it indispensable that an arm of war should be susceptible of being used whenever powder and lead can be obtained. As to caps, they are so cheap and abundant that they can be procured at all times and in any quantity, especially when we have established a state manufactory of military caps. With volunteers and militia, who cannot have always within their reach the advantage of regular magazines, it is of the utmost importance that they should be able to prepare their own ammunition at all times without any difficulty. We need weapons of such a character, that if the citizen soldiers are suddenly called to arms, every man, with the powder and lead he can procure at the next country store, will be ready for action, and not find himself paralzed for having lost some india rubber or brass cartridge cases. I would earnestly press upon the commission the consideration that all arms requiring complicated ammunition or apparatus, are unfit for military service, and especially for ours.

With regard to the peculiar mode of breaking off of Smith & Poultney's carbine—I consider it inferior, as to the facility and quickness of loading to Burnside's and Maynard's. I am much accustomed to using fire arms on horseback. and have tried all these arms in that way. If Smith's gun be placed in the hollow of the arm for loading, it deranges the position of the bridle hand, and at last, the gun has to be placed in this hand for priming, for I believe it will be generally conceded that Maynard's priming apparatus is unsatisfactory. This causes a loss of time. There is a further loss of time in loading, by having to remove an empty case, even if only to let it drop on the ground. It is my belief that not one empty case would ever be saved to be used a second time, in active service. In all the firing I did on horseback, I let them fall to the ground.

BURNSIDE'S CARBINE.—This is a beautiful arm, shoots admirably, loads quickly. and does not foul. The cartridges are brass, and the arm would be useless without them. All the objections above mentioned apply here; also that of the high price of the arm. There is, moreover, danger that in the hurry of loading, a cartridge may be put into the chamber without withdrawing the empty case. There is no escape of gas in this gun.

MAYNARD'S RIFLE.—This arm is extremely powerful, considering its dimensions, but from my experiments with it. it does not realize what is claimed for it. Its make is utterly unsuited for military service, being entirely too delicate and too light. The mode in which the sight is fixed is very objectionable. It would be very easy to remedy many of these faults, by fitting it with a heavier stock (with rings,) which would afford the means of slinging it, and would diminish its recoil, at the same time adding to its solidity; also by fixing a different kind of sight to the barrel instead of the stock. The objection to the price would still remain. As for the loading, the same remarks apply as above. The arm is useless without a brass cartridge, or at least a loader. With this brass loader, the arm may be used with loose power and ball or paper cartridge; but this brass loader being detached from the piece, is too easy to lose. There is no escape of gas in this gun nor fouling at the breech. Of all the arms which I have tried which load with a peculiar cartridge case, I think the principle of breaking off of this one is the best. This arm missed fire a number of times.

MERRILL'S BREECH-LOADING ARMS.—Mr. Merrill claims no other advantage for his arms than the method of breech-loading. This may be applied to any barrels. Among the arms submitted, are a U. S. musket and a U. S. Harper's Ferry rifle altered to breech-loading by this process.

I have no hesitation in saying, that of all the breech-loading arms I have seen, these seem to me the best suited for the purposes we have in view, and for the following reasons:

CHEAPNESS.—The inventor offers no arms for sale. We are not, therefore, obliged to buy his guns at his own price, as we would have to do if we bought the Burnsides or the Maynard. The guns can be made of any kind we choose at our armory, and very little additional machinery would be required to make the breech-loading apparatus. The unlimited right of using the process by the state armory might be purchased from the inventor, or else a fixed sum paid him for each arm thus manufactured; and unless he charged extravagantly for the privilege, the additional cost to each arm would be small. I should suppose that a cavalry carbine of the same calibre as the musket or rifle, to be made at the armory, and having an effective range of at least 600 yards, might be made with Merrill's improvement, at a cost not over $10—but this is a mere conjecture, and would depend entirely on what the inventor charged.

SOLIDITY.—Merrill's arrangement seems to offer great strength, and to be able to stand heavy charges. There does not seem to be any friction between the parts, which can lead to rapid wearing.

SIMPLICITY.—The breech-loading apparatus is very simple, and easy to take to pieces and put together again for cleaning or oiling. I have not been able to detect any escape of gas. After firing over 100 shots, I wiped the piston rod with a white pocket handkerchief, and found not the slightest trace of powder or dirt.

AMMUNITION.—The great advantage of these arms over the others is, that they can be used with the paper cartridge or with loose powder and ball, without any metallic or other cartridge case. This secures one of the indispensible conditions of an arm of war.

Another advantage of Mr. Merrill's patent is the ease with which it may be applied to other arms. Take for example the U. S. Minnie rifle altered by him. It has the same barrel, stock and lock. Nothing is removed but the old breech screw, and the arm is not in the least degree diminished in solidity, and hardly changed at all in appearance. It must be added to this, that this altered arm seemed to have the same range and force with 50 grains of powder as the unaltered rifle with the regular charge of 60 grains.

If it should be thought advisable to give breech-loading carbines to cavalry, and breech-loading muskets and rifles to the sergeants of infantry, I would give the preference, so far as I am able to judge, to Mr. Merrill's arms. But I must say that the experiments performed hitherto, while they induce me to give a positive opinion *against* certain arms, do not enable me to pronounce as positively in favor of any. As to the Minnie arms, we have sufficient testimony in the reports of American and foreign officers. With regard to Mr. Merrill's arms, they have borne successfully the test of a few hundred shots. But they must be fired several thousand times at least, before a conclusive opinion can be formed.

The experiments in which I have been engaged were commenced only a few weeks ago, and carried on only during the leisure hours left me by other duties. I did not expect to present a report of them until they were finished, and they ought to extend over a period of several months. This report is therefore necessarily very incomplete, for not half the arms have been tried that ought to be. Moreover, having to draw it up during the labors of the institute examinations, its imperfections are the greater for this cause. I hope that the commission will overlook them, and also that I may be able at a future period to offer them a report less unworthy of their attention.

Extract of a Letter from ALFRED M. BARBOUR, Esq., *Superintendent, U. S. Harper's Ferry Armory.*

HARPER'S FERRY, VA., *Jan.* 15*th*, 1861.

Messrs. MERRILL, THOMAS & CO.

GENTLEMEN:

* * * * * * * * * * * * * *

Please send my gun.

Will you let me know whether 1000 or 2000 of your guns can be purchased, and at what price. I have just recommended your gun.

Yours respectfully,

(Signed) ALFRED M. BARBOUR.

———

Extract of a Letter from P. BURKHART, Esq., *Inspector of Arms, U. S. Armory, Harper's Ferry.*

HARPER'S FERRY ARMORY, *Oct.* 12*th*, 1861.

GENTLEMEN:

* * * * * * * * * * * * * *

The Topic of Breech-loading Arms, occupies no small portion of men's attention here, as elsewhere; of this fact I am sure you are fully aware, but you may not be aware of the extreme ignorance that exists in this section of country in regard to the very existence of your gun.

Now my object in mentioning this, is simply to say to you, that you are wholly unrepresented here, and why should this be so?

You fully know my opinion in regard to it. You further know, or at least ought to, that I expect nothing from you in any shape or form, (save a good will,) but am purely actuated from a positive conviction that your gun will fully sustain itself against any other, having the advantage of great simplicity, and the additional advantage of being fired with or without fixed ammunition. Send therefore one of your guns of fair finish, to represent your case, and whenever you desire its return, indicate the same to me. In conclusion, permit me to hope, that you will regard my foregoing recommendation in the same light that it is meant.

I am, Sir,

Your obedient Servant,

(Signed) P. BURKHART.

4 0

11

Letter from Captain R. E. Robinson, *of the 1st Cavalry, Petersburg, Va., whose Company is armed with the Merrill Carbine.*

Petersburg, Virginia, *March* 5, 1861.

Your letter of the 2nd inst. came to hand this morning, and I have been too constantly engaged all day to reply sooner.

You have requested me to give you my opinion of your construction for Breech-Loading Arms, and I have no hesitation in saying, that no commendation would be necessary where they could be submitted to examination, for in all such cases they would speak for themselves. The best authorities in the English service have pronounced, that finally breech-loaders must carry the day over all muzzle-loaders, as may be seen by referring to Hans Busk's work, "The Rifle, and how to use it," Sixth Ed., page 111. And it cannot be denied that no breech-loader, now known, combines to the same extent that yours does, all the requisites as an arm for service. Its simplicity and strength are unequaled; it can be thoroughly cleaned *without turning a screw*, unless it should be necessary to remove the lock; there is not the *slightest* escape of gas in firing it; the soldier can, in any position, load and discharge it with perfect ease, and should the fixed ammunition be expended, it is equally effective when loaded with loose powder and ball, no patch or wadding being required! This peculiarity needs no comment—it is, in my opinion, an indispensable requisite. Another great advantage of your patent is, that it can be applied readily, and at little expense, to any other arms, and without diminishing their solidity and strength in the slightest degree. Moreover, in all such cases, it has been found that the altered arm has the same range and force with a smaller charge of powder. Under these circumstances, I have no hesitation in saying, that I believe it to be the best arm in use at this day.

In haste, I remain yours truly,

R. E. Robinson,

Capt. 1st Cavalry, Va.

To the Secretary of the Merrill Patent
Fire Arm Co., Baltimore.

From the Baltimore Exchange.

The Merrill Patent Arm Manufactory.—It is worth being generally known, that there is now in successful operation in Baltimore a manufactory of Breech-Loading Arms, on a principle invented and patented by one of our own citizens, Mr. James Merrill, which, in some very important particulars, appears to be superior to that used in any other gun. "The advantage that Merrill's

Breech-Loading Rifles have over other breech-loading arms are, (says a recent official report:) 1. *Solidity*. Merrill's arrangement seems to offer great strength, and to be able to stand heavy charges. There does not seem to be any friction between the parts which can lead to wearing. 2. *Simplicity*. The Breech-Loading Apparatus is very simple, easy to take to pieces and put together again for cleaning or oiling; after firing one hundred shots, I wiped the piston with a white pocket-handkerchief, and found not the slightest trace of powder or dirt. 3. *Ammunition*. The great advantage of these arms over the others is, that they can be used with the paper cartridge or loose powder and ball, without any metallic or other cartridge case. This seems one of the most indispensable conditions for arms of war. Another advantage of Mr. Merrill's Patent is the ease with which it may be applied to other arms. Take for example, the U. S. *Minnie* Rifles, altered by him; it has the same barrel-stock and lock, nothing is removed but the old breech-screw, and the arm is not in the least diminished in solidity, and hardly changed at all in appearance. It must be added to this, that this altered arm seems to have the same range and force, with fifty grains of powder, as the unaltered rifle, with the regular charge of sixty grains."

This Company, chartered by the last Legislature, have taken the two upper stories of the Sun Iron Building, and have already erected a large part of their machinery—for which power is supplied by the engine on the premises. Any one who takes pleasure in witnessing the perfection of processes performed—with a perfection that the human hand can never equal—by machinery alone, would be gratified by an inspection of the several machines now in operation upon these premises. In all the great modern manufactories of arms, the many pieces constituting them are reproduced as perfect fac-similes, so that any loss of the smallest piece can be at once supplied. To effect this, it is absolutely necessary to employ machinery of the most curious and complicated description, and it may really be said that the machinery by which the requisite tools are produced, and the different parts of a gun constructed, are themselves even more wonderful and ingenious than the instruments they are at work upon. This Company are supplying themselves with all that modern art can afford to render their arms as perfect in construction, as they are valuable in principle, and in a very short time we shall be able to boast of a Southern manufactory of a Rifle of Southern invention, very far superior to Sharpe's celebrated patent. The Company has just completed a large order for the United States Government, of altering a number of Harper's Ferry Minnie Rifles from muzzle to breech-loaders—it being one of the peculiarities of this principle, that it can be readily and economically applied to any of the old-fashioned government arms.

From the Patapsco Enterprise.

Experiments with Fire-arms.—The numerous military companies that have lately been organized in the different counties of the State, having been well officered and uniformed, have all been much interested of late in the experiments made before them by the inventors and agents of improved fire-arms. So far, wherever tried, in comparison with every other arm, Merrill's Patent Breech-Loading Carbine seems to have carried off the palm. A series of experiments were also made at this place on Saturday last, before a committee of the Howard Dragoons, with a view to the adoption of the Patent Breech-Loading Carbine, invented by Mr. James H. Merrill, of the firm of Merrill, Thomas & Co., of Baltimore. The Carbine presented only weighs six pounds, and is so well proportioned, that it feels like a feather in the hand, and can easily be used with one hand. Light as it is, it made its mark on Saturday last on the tree it peppered at half a mile distant. One hundred and fifty shots were fired from the carbine with great rapidity and accuracy, without any change taking place in the working of the machinery of the gun, which is of the most simple construction, and not liable to get out of order. After firing the above number of shots, scarcely more dirt was found in the barrel than the first shot left, and no clogging or leading took place, and not one misfire. We feel satisfied that any number of shots could have been fired without cleaning it. The committee expressed itself highly pleased with the trial, and will no doubt at the next meeting recommend its adoption by the Company. Mr. Merrill also presented for trial, one of his Breech-Loading Rifled Muskets, which gave complete satisfaction to some of our townsmen, who think of getting up the Infantry Company, of which there was so much talk last fall. We recommend all Companies who wish to keep up with the progress of the age, and who do not wish to have the sobriquet of "old fogy" attached to their Company, to adopt the "Merrill Breech-Loader," and feel sure that those who do, will have the most efficient military fire-arm in use.

———

From the Philadelphia Sunday Mercury.

The Military.—In last week's *Mercury* we gave a short description of Merrill's Breech-Loading Musket. On Wednesday last, in company with Col. F. E. Patterson, Major D. P. Weaver, Brevet Major Peter Lyle, Major Wm. A. Delaney, and Capt. Archambault, of the Pennsylvania volunteer troops, Mr. Merrill, the Inventor of the Breech-Loading Rifle, and Major T. Sparks, of the Maryland militia, we proceeded by way of the Philadelphia, Wilmington and Baltimore Railroad to the Lazaretto, on the Delaware River, for the purpose of giving the guns a trial.

Three guns were tried, a small carbine, weighing six pounds, intended for cavalry; an ordinary musket, which had been altered by Mr. Merrill; and a Dahlgren musket, which had also been altered, all being charged at the breech.

The pieces all stood the severest test, the small carbine being fired upwards of one hundred and thirty times. It threw a ball across the channel to the island opposite, a distance of three quarters of a mile. The Dahlgren gun and the ordinary musket, were both fired down the river to a point of the island, about one and three-quarters or two miles distant, and each carried a ball clear over it. The distances was only estimated, but they were no doubt correct, as they were obtained from the fishermen, who are familiar with every foot of ground in the vicinity. The shots at the distance were fired at random, but upon selecting some mark, the guns were found to carry with remarkable accuracy, striking within a few feet of the place intended.

A temporary target, a piece of board, about eight inches wide, by four feet long, was placed on the shore, at six hundred yards distance, and all hands took several shots at it. Only three balls pierced it, but nearly every one went so close to it that if the figure of a man had been there it would have been riddled. A small target was next made, and placed against the wharf, and the party fired at it at fifty yards and one hundred yards. At fifty yards poor shooting was made, the distance being too close. At one hundred yards it was excellent, and Capt. Lyle put half a dozen balls in the little target, two of them touching the bull's eye. Col. Patterson was the next best shot, his "string" being little behind that of Capt. Lyle.

The rapidity with which the pieces were fired was really surprising. As fast as one load was discharged, the lever at the breech was raised, another cartridge inserted, a cap put on the nipple, and the piece was ready to be fired again. In this way one of these rifles can be discharged ten times a minute; but if fired so rapidly, the barrel becomes so much heated, that it is unpleasant to handle. But it may be fired five or six times a minute without inconvenience.

The advantages claimed for Merrill's Invention over the Minnie Rifles are, that while it will carry a ball as far, it can be loaded and fired with greater rapidity, the "ramming" of the cartridge being entirely dispensed with, which saves several "motions" now required by troops in loading.

A very ingenious arrangement of the piece is that, after it is discharged, on raising the lever to reload, the exploded cap is taken off, leaving the nipple ready for another cap.

The opinion of the officers who tested the pieces was, that they are a great improvement over the latest improved muskets—even the Minnie. One of the pieces has been left at Gen. Cadwalader's office, Eleventh and Chesnut streets, where our military men would do well to call and look at it. Several officers have examined the piece who have not seen it tried, and they fully agree with those who tested it.

We have extended our remarks on this subject to some length, as our desire is to get our volunteers interested in the matter. We are informed, that if a movement is made among the officers, in the shape of a memorial to Congress, there is a probability that all our troops can receive the improved arms, before the present Congress adjourns. This can be done without the usual way of making a requisition to the Adjutant General of the State. All of us know what we have suffered for want of arms, and how difficult it is to get any. Let us then commence this movement now, and show for once that Philadelphia is "wide awake," and in advance of her neighbors. Heretofore we have always been in the back ground, while our neighbors of New York, particularly the Seventh Regiment, enjoys a national reputation, and why? simply because they are always looking out for No. 1, and "God always helps those who help themselves." Get up at once, then, your memorials and petitions, to be supplied with the new arms. Mr. Longnecker, of this State, is on the Military Committee of the House, and will no doubt do all in his power to grant the wishes of the memorialists. The weapon is no untried affair, but has stood the severest tests of army and navy officers, and the patentees are now filling a large order for the U. S. army.

www.ingramcontent.com/pod-product-compliance
Lightning Source LLC
Chambersburg PA
CBHW022148090426
42742CB00010B/1427